AF568147

AGRICULTURAL IMPORTANCE OF SEEDS

AGRICULTURAL IMPORTANCE OF SEEDS

By

Dr. Renuka Sharma

DISCOVERY PUBLISHING HOUSE PVT. LTD.

NEW DELHI-110 002

Published by:

Tilak Wasan

DISCOVERY PUBLISHING HOUSE PVT. LTD.

4383/4B, Ansari Road, Darya Ganj

New Delhi-110 002 (India)

Phone : +91-11-23279245, 43596064-65

Fax : +91-11-23253475

E-mail : parul.wasan@gmail.com
discoverypublishinghouse@gmail.com

web : www.discoverypublishinggroup.com

***First Edition:* 2014**

ISBN: 978-93-5056-402-8

Agricultural Importance of Seeds

Printed at:

Dynamic Printers

Delhi

Preface

Seed is a fundamental input for agriculture. Indeed, seed is the single most important input in all crop-based farming systems and a prerequisite for most of the world's food production. More than being the basis of production for the majority of the world's crops, seed determines the upper limit on yield and therefore on the ultimate productivity of all other inputs.

Seeds have been an important development in the reproduction and spread of flowering plants, relative to more primitive plants like mosses, ferns and liverworts, which do not have seeds and use other means to propagate themselves. This can be seen by the success of seed plants (both gymnosperms and angiosperms) in dominating biological niches on land, from forests to grasslands both in hot and cold climates.

The seed of most legume species contains a high proportion of 'hard seeds'. The seed coat of such seeds will not allow the seed to take up moisture and thus to germinate unless it is treated in some way. In the longer term, hard seed will germinate because of the influence of changes in soil temperature and moisture content on the seed coat but with some species this may take several years. For a rapid germination and establishment of seed of less than 9 months of age, seed should be treated either by mechanical scarification or by immersion in hot water -both techniques readily suited to commercial practice.

There are often techniques, such as heat treatment or acid scarification but which are more difficult to undertake, especially for large quantities of seed and the lack of appropriate facilities for on farm treatments.

Mechanical scarification can be carried out by abrasing seed with sandpaper in a rotating drum lined with medium grain sandpaper and fitted with a spinning disc that throws seed against the walls of the container. Small quantities of seed can be treated by rubbing the seed between sandpaper. Rubbing seed on a rough cement floor is also effective.

Cultivar purity is the first consideration in seed certification, but other factors such as the absence of weeds and diseases, viability, mechanical purity, and grade are also important. One of the most effective ways to limit the distribution of weeds is to plant weed-free seed. Planting disease-free seed can reduce losses in the same way.

Properly, cleaned and graded seed is easier to plant and gives more uniform stand. Thus, seed certification has been designed not only to maintain genetic purity of superior cultivars, but also to establish and maintain reasonable standards of seed condition and quality.

—Author

Contents

1 Introduction

Seed is a living product that must be grown, harvested and processed correctly to maximize its viability and subsequent crop productivity. For the yield potential of any rice variety to be realized, good quality seed must be sown. Good quality seed can increase yields by 5-20 per cent. The extent of this increase is directly proportional to the quality of seed that is being sown. Seed quality can be considered as the summation of all factors that contribute to seed performance.

High quality seed enables farmers to attain crops, which have:

- the most economical planting rate;
- a higher percentage of seeds;
- emerging in the field;
- a minimum of replanting;
- a vigorous seedling establishment;
- a more uniform plant stand;
- faster growth rate;
- greater resistance to stress and diseases; and
- uniformity in ripening.

Seed quality is determined by a number of genetic and physiological characteristics. The genetic component involves differences between two or more genetic lines, while differences between seed lots of a single genetic line comprise the physiological component.

The genetic factors that can influence quality include:

- genetic make-up;
- seed size; and
- bulk density.

The physical or environmental characteristics include:

- injury during planting and establishment;
- growing conditions during seed development;
- nutrition of the mother plant;
- physical damage during production or storage by either machine or pest;
- moisture and temperature during storage; and
- age or maturity of seed.

Deterioration in seed quality may begin at any point in the plant's development stage from fertilization onward. Seed quality depends upon the physical conditions that the mother plant is exposed during its growth stages, as well as harvesting, processing, storage and planting. Temperature, nutrients and other environmental factors also affect seed development and influence seed quality.

High quality seeds are the result of good production practices, which include:

- proper maintenance of genetic purity;
- good growing conditions;
- proper timing and methods of harvesting;
- appropriate processing during threshing, cleaning and drying;
- appropriate seed storage and seed distribution systems.

Seed Certification

The purpose of seed certification is to maintain and make available to farmers, high quality and genetically pure seeds of superior cultivars. Only those cultivars that are of superior genetic makeup, multiplied to maintain purity and identity, are normally eligible for government certification. Certified seed is high in genetic purity, high in germination and vigour, and of good quality (i.e., free from disease and from damaged or immature seeds).

Cultivar purity is the first consideration in seed certification, but other factors such as the absence of weeds and diseases, viability, mechanical purity, and grade are also important. One of the most effective ways to limit the distribution of weeds is to plant weed-free seed. Planting disease-free seed can reduce losses in the same way.

Properly, cleaned and graded seed is easier to plant and gives more uniform stand. Thus, seed certification has been designed not only to maintain genetic purity of superior cultivars, but also to establish and maintain reasonable standards of seed condition and quality.

Seed Testing

Seed samples are collected and submitted for laboratory analysis after drying and processing.

Tests conducted include:

- Varietal purity;
- Weed and other crop seed;
- Inert material;
- Other varieties;
- Red rice;
- Germination; and
- Moisture content.

For seed certification, field inspectors must check:

- Crop land requirements (e.g., previous crop and isolation distances to ensure no pollen mixes and or volunteers from a different previously planted cultivar).
- The source of the crop's seed (to ensure cultivar purity).
- Sowing dates, pattern, spacing, and rouging (to ensure crop kept clean and free from contamination).
- Purity of cultivar (i.e., no cultivar mixes).

- Harvesting methods (to prevent mixtures).
- Postharvest operations to ensure correct cleaning, drying, sampling, tagging, labeling and sealing.

Seed Management

This section covers important aspects of seed management. One of the main reasons for failure or partial success of establishment of improved pastures involves inadequate soil seed contact, use of poor quality seed and insufficient quantities of viable seed sown per hectare. The cost of seed represents usually 10 per cent to 20 per cent of pasture development costs and it is short sighted to compromise the seeding operation.

Seed Treatment

The seed of most legume species contains a high proportion of 'hard seeds'. The seed coat of such seeds will not allow the seed to take up moisture and thus to germinate unless it is treated in some way. In the longer term, hard seed will germinate because of the influence of changes in soil temperature and moisture content on the seed coat but with some species this may take several years. For a rapid germination and establishment of seed of less than 9 months of age, seed should be treated either by mechanical scarification or by immersion in hot water - both techniques readily suited to commercial practice.

There are often techniques, such as heat treatment or acid scarification but which are more difficult to undertake, especially for large quantities of seed and the lack of appropriate facilities for on farm treatments.

Mechanical scarification can be carried out by abrasing seed with sandpaper in a rotating drum lined with medium grain sandpaper and fitted with a spinning disc that throws seed against the walls of the container. Small quantities of seed can be treated by rubbing the seed between sandpaper. Rubbing seed on a rough cement floor is also effective.

The alternative is to heat seed in water at 80°C for four minutes and allowing it to dry out. This is the specific recommendation for leucaena seed if less than 12 months old.

Some grasses, particularly signal and Sabi grass require a post harvest period of 9-12 months before providing a high content of viable seed.

Seed Storage

Storage temperature and seed moisture content are the most important factors influencing the deterioration of stored seed.

This is especially important for grass seed where high temperatures and high humidity can quickly reduce seed viability. For instance recorded signal grass germinations have declined from 60 per cent on arrival in Vanuatu in January to 30 per cent in April in cool, non-airconditioned storage. Even under air-conditioning in Vanuatu grass seed should not be stored for more than 3 months, otherwise the quality of pasture establishment will decline.

For short term storage (1-9 months) the temperature and per cent relative humidity should not exceed 30°C and 50 per cent RH or 20°C and 60 per cent RH; for intermediate storage (9-18 months) the ranges are 30°C, 40 per cent RH; or 20°C and 50 per cent RH or 10°C and 60 per cent RH.

On farm seed should be stored in a cool, dry, ventilated room with aluminium reflective insulation under the roof. Seed bags should be off the floor and the area should be rat proof..

When purchasing seed insist on information from a recent seed quality analysis from a recognised laboratory. Always buy the highest germination line possible because this will give you the greatest number of established seedlings for your investment.

New conditions apply for permission to import seed into Vanuatu. This is essential as in excess of 30 tonnes of seed per annum is imported and there are risks of introducing new undesirable weeds or seed of totally unacceptable weeds that already exist here. Also there are risks of introducing live insects.

For longer term storage of small quantities of seed, packages of laminated materials such as layers of polythene, aluminium foil, cellophane or polyester should be used. Polythene alone transmits water vapour and is not recommended for seed storage under high temperature and humidity conditions.

Rhizobial Requirements of Legumes

Most legumes require inoculation with rhizobia that will enable the plants to fix nitrogen from the air. In many cases a specific strain of rhizobium is required e.g. for centro seed, but in others the soil may contain the appropriate rhizobium and inoculation may not be required.

However, even if the soil contains the required rhizobium strain the rate of nodulation and nitrogen fixation will be increased through applying the inoculant in contact with the seed.

The rhizobium is commercially available mixed in a peat culture, which ensures the survival of the rhizobia until seed germination. Improved survival is obtained by using an adhesive or sticker to attach the inoculum to the seed. The most readily available form of sticker is a 10 per cent sugar solution (i.e. 10 gm sugar in 100 ml water). Seed is wetted with the solution and the peat culture mixed with the seed and allowed to dry in the shade - direct sunlight will kill the rhizobium.

The main points to be observed when inoculating seed are:

- make sure that the seed has not been treated with chemical and that containers used do not contain toxic substances such as oil, petrol, chemical pesticides;

- do not mix inoculated seed with acid fertilisers such as superphosphate;
- ensure that the peat culture used is within the expiry period;
- store inoculum in a refrigerator - up to 2 months maximum.
- sow into moist soil.

Spraying a peat/inoculum mix onto established legumes during cloudy weather can partially or completely overcome nodulation failure.

2 What is a Seed ?

A seed is a small embryonic plant enclosed in a covering called the seed coat, usually with some stored food. It is the product of the ripened ovule of gymnosperm and angiosperm plants which occurs after fertilization and some growth within the mother plant. The formation of the seed completes the process of reproduction in seed plants (started with the development of flowers and pollination), with the embryo developed from the zygote and the seed coat from the integuments of the ovule.

Seeds have been an important development in the reproduction and spread of flowering plants, relative to more primitive plants like mosses, ferns and liverworts, which do not have seeds and use other means to propagate themselves. This can be seen by the success of seed plants (both gymnosperms and angiosperms) in dominating biological niches on land, from forests to grasslands both in hot and cold climates.

The term *seed* also has a general meaning that predates the above — anything that can be sown, e.g. “seed” potatoes, “seeds” of corn or sunflower “seeds”. In the case of sunflower and corn “seeds”, what is sown is the seed enclosed in a shell or hull, and the potato is a tuber.

A typical seed includes three basic parts:

1. an embryo;
2. a supply of nutrients for the embryo; and
3. a seed coat.

The embryo is an immature plant from which a new plant will grow under proper conditions. The embryo has one cotyledon or seed leaf in monocotyledons, two cotyledons in almost all dicotyledons and two or more in gymnosperms. The radicle is the embryonic root. The plumule is the embryonic shoot. The embryonic stem above the point of attachment of the cotyledon(s) is the epicotyl. The embryonic stem below the point of attachment is the hypocotyl.

Within the seed, there usually is a store of nutrients for the seedling that will grow from the embryo. The form of the stored nutrition varies depending on the kind of plant. In angiosperms, the stored food begins as a tissue called the endosperm, which is derived from the parent plant via double fertilization. The usually triploid endosperm is rich in oil or starch and protein. In gymnosperms, such as conifers, the food storage tissue is part of the female gametophyte, a haploid tissue. In some species, the embryo is embedded in the endosperm or female gametophyte, which the seedling will use upon germination. In others, the endosperm is absorbed by the embryo as the latter grows within the developing seed, and the cotyledons of the embryo become filled with this stored food. At maturity, seeds of these species have no endosperm and are termed exalbuminous seeds. Some exalbuminous seeds are bean, pea, oak, walnut, squash, sunflower, and radish. Seeds with an endosperm at maturity are termed albuminous seeds. Most monocots (e.g. grasses and palms) and many dicots (e.g. brazil nut and castor bean) have albuminous seeds. All gymnosperm seeds are albuminous.

The seed coat (or *testa*) develops from the tissue, the integument, originally surrounding the ovule. The seed coat in the mature seed can be a paper-thin layer (e.g. peanut) or something more substantial (e.g. thick and hard in honey locust and coconut). The seed coat helps protect the embryo from mechanical injury and from drying out.

In addition to the three basic seed parts, some seeds have an appendage on the seed coat such an aril (as in yew and nutmeg) or an elaiosome (as in Corydalis) or hairs (as in cotton). There may also be a scar on the seed coat, called the hilum; it is where the seed was attached to the ovary wall by the funiculus.

Seeds are produced in several related groups of plants, and their manner of production distinguishes the angiosperms ("enclosed seeds") from the gymnosperms ("naked seeds"). Angiosperm seeds are produced in a hard or fleshy structure called a fruit that encloses the seeds, hence the name. (Some fruits have layers of both hard and fleshy material). In gymnosperms, no special structure develops to enclose the seeds, which begin their development "naked" on the bracts of cones. However, the seeds do become covered by the cone scales as they develop in some species of conifer.

Seed production in natural plant populations vary widely from year-to-year in response to weather variables, insects and diseases, and internal cycles within the plants themselves. Over a 20-year period, for example, forests composed of loblolly pine and shortleaf pine produced from 0 to nearly 5 million sound pine seeds per hectare. Over this period, there were six bumper seeds, five poor seeds crops, and nine good seed crops, when evaluated in regard to producing adequate seedlings for natural forest reproduction.

Kinds of Seeds

Many structures commonly referred to as "seeds" are actually dry fruits. Sunflower seeds are sold commercially while still enclosed within the hard wall of the fruit, which must be split open to reach the seed. Different groups of plants have other modifications, the so-called *stone* fruits (such as the peach) have a hardened fruit layer (the endocarp) fused to and surrounding the actual seed. Nuts are the one-seeded, hard shelled fruit, of some plants, with an indehiscent seed, such as an acorn or hazelnut.

Seed Development

The seed, which is an embryo with two points of growth (one of which forms the stems the other the roots) is enclosed in a seed coat with some food reserves. Angiosperm seeds consist of three genetically distinct constituents:

1. the embryo formed from the zygote;
2. the endosperm, which is normally triploid;
3. the seed coat from tissue derived from the maternal tissue of the ovule.

In angiosperms, the process of seed development begins with double fertilization and involves the fusion of the egg and sperm nuclei into a zygote. The second part of this process is the fusion of the polar nuclei with a second sperm cell nucleus, thus forming a primary endosperm. Right after fertilization, the zygote is mostly inactive but the primary endosperm divides rapidly to form the endosperm tissue. This tissue becomes the food that the young plant will consume until the roots have developed after germination or it develops into a hard seed coat. The seed coat forms from the two integuments or outer layers of cells of the ovule, which derive from tissue from the mother plant, the inner integument forms the tegmen and the outer forms the testa. When the seed coat forms from only one layer it is also called the testa, though not all such testa are homologous from one species to the next.

In gymnosperms, the two sperm cells transferred from the pollen do not develop seed by double fertilization but one sperm nucleus unites with the egg nucleus and the other sperm is not used. Sometimes each sperm fertilizes an egg cell and one zygote is then aborted or absorbed during early development. The seed is composed of the embryo (the result of fertilization) and tissue from the mother plant, which also form a cone around the seed in coniferous plants like Pine and Spruce.

The ovules after fertilization develop into the seeds; the main parts of the ovule are the funicle; which attaches the ovule to the placenta, the nucellus; the main region of the ovule were the embryo sac develops, the micropyle; A small pore or opening in the ovule where the pollen tube usually enters during the process of fertilization, and the chalaza; the base of the ovule opposite the micropyle, where integument and nucellus are joined together.

The shape of the ovules as they develop often affects the finale shape of the seeds. Plants generally produce ovules of four shapes: the most common shape is called anatropous, with a curved shape. Orthotropous ovules are straight with all the parts of the ovule lined up in a long row producing an uncurved seed. Campylotropous ovules have a curved embryo sac often giving the seed a tight "c" shape. The last ovule shape is called amphitropous, where the ovule is partly inverted and turned back 90 degrees on its stalk or funicle. In the majority of flowering plants, the zygote's first division is transversely oriented in regards to the long axis, and this establishes the polarity of the embryo. The upper or chalazal pole becomes the main area of growth of the embryo, while the lower or micropylar pole produces the stalk-like suspensor that attaches to the micropyle. The suspensor absorbs and manufacturers nutrients from the endosperm that are utilized during the embryos growth.

The embryo is composed of different parts; the epicotyle will grow into the shoot, the radicle grows into the primary root, the hypocotyl connects the epicotyle and the radicle, the cotyledons form the seed leaves, the testa or seed coat forms the outer covering of the seed. Monocotyledonous plants like corn, have other structures; instead of the hypocotyle-epicotyle, it has a coleoptile that forms the first leaf and connects to the coleorhiza that connects to the primary root and adventitious roots form from the sides. The seeds of corn are constructed with these structures; pericarp, scutellum (single large cotyledon) that absorbs nutrients from the endosperm, endosperm, plumule, radicle, coleoptile and coleorhiza - these last two structures are sheath-like and enclose the plumule and radicle, acting as a protective covering. The testa or seed coats of both monocots and dicots are often marked with patterns and textured markings, or have wings or tufts of hair.

Seed Size and Seed Set

Seeds are very diverse in size. The dust-like orchid seeds are the smallest with about one million seeds per gram; they are often embryonic seeds with immature embryos and no significant energy reserves. Orchids and a few other groups of plants are myco-heterotrophs which depend on mycorrhizal fungi for nutrition during germination and the early growth of the seedling. Some terrestrial Orchid seedlings, in fact, spend the first few years of their life deriving energy from the fungus and do not produce green leaves. At over 20 kg, the largest seed is the coco de mer. Plants that produce smaller seeds can generate many more seeds per flower, while plants with larger seeds invest more resources into those seeds and normally produce fewer seeds. Small seeds are quicker to ripen and can be dispersed sooner, so fall blooming plants often have small seeds. Many annual plants produce great quantities of smaller seeds; this helps to ensure that at least a few will end in a favourable place for growth. Herbaceous perennials and woody plants often have larger seeds, they can produce seeds over many years, and larger seeds have more energy reserves for germination and seedling growth and produce larger, more established seedlings after germination.

Seed Functions

Seeds serve several functions for the plants that produce them. Key among these functions are nourishment of the embryo, dispersal to a new location, and dormancy during unfavorable conditions. Seeds fundamentally are a means of reproduction and most seeds are the product of sexual reproduction which produces a remixing of genetic material and phenotype variability that natural selection acts on.

Embryo Nourishment

Seeds protect and nourish the embryo or young plant. Seeds usually give a seedling a faster start than a sporeling from a spore, because of the larger food reserves in the seed and the multicellularity of the enclosed embryo.

Seed Dispersal

Unlike animals, plants are limited in their ability to seek out favorable conditions for life and growth. As a result, plants have evolved many ways to disperse their offspring by dispersing their seeds. A seed must somehow "arrive" at a location and be there at a time favorable for germination and growth. When the fruits open and release their seeds in a regular way, it is called dehiscent, which is often distinctive for related groups of plants, these fruits include; Capsules, follicles, legumes, silicles and siliques. When fruits do not open and release their seeds in a regular fashion they are called indehiscent, which include the fruits achenes, caryopsis, nuts, samaras, and utricles.

Seed dispersal is seen most obviously in fruits; however many seeds aid in their own dispersal. Some kinds of seeds are dispersed while still inside a fruit or cone, which later opens or disintegrates to release the seeds. Other seeds are expelled or released from the fruit prior to dispersal. For example, milkweeds produce a fruit type, known as a *follicle*, that splits open along one side to release the seeds. Iris capsules split into three "valves" to release their seeds.

By Wind (Anemochory)

- The seed pod of milkweed (Asclepias syriaca)
- Many seeds (e.g. maple, pine) have a wing that aids in wind dispersal.
- The dustlike seeds of orchids are carried efficiently by the wind.
- Some seeds, (e.g. dandelion, milkweed, poplar) have hairs that aid in wind dispersal.
- Some winged seeds have two, and some have only one wing.

By Water (Hydrochory)

- Some plants, such as *Mucuna* and *Dioclea*, produce buoyant seeds termed sea-beans or drift seeds because they float in rivers to the oceans and wash up on beaches.

By Animals (Zoochory)

- Seeds (burrs) with barbs or hooks (e.g. acaena, burdock, dock) which attach to animal fur or feathers, and then drop off later.
- Seeds with a fleshy covering (e.g. apple, cherry, juniper) are eaten by animals (birds, mammals, reptiles, fish) which then disperse these seeds in their droppings.
- Seeds (nuts) which are an attractive long-term storable food resource for animals (e.g. acorns, hazelnut, walnut); the seeds are stored some distance from the parent plant, and some escape being eaten if the animal forgets them.

Myrmecochory is the dispersal of seeds by ants. Foraging ants disperse seeds which have appendages called elaiosomes (e.g. bloodroot, trilliums, Acacias, and many species of Proteaceae). Elaiosomes are soft, fleshy structures that contain nutrients for animals that eat them. The ants carry such seeds back to their nest, where the elaiosomes are eaten. The remainder of the seed, which is hard and inedible to the ants, then germinates either within the nest or at a removal site where the seed has been discarded by the ants. This dispersal relationship is an example of mutualism, since the plants depend upon the ants to disperse seeds, while the ants depend upon the plants seeds for food. As a result, a drop in numbers of one partner can reduce success of the other. In South Africa, the Argentine ant (*Linepithema humile*) has invaded and displaced native species of ants. Unlike the native ant species, Argentine ants do not collect the seeds of *Mimetes cucullatus* or eat the elaiosomes. In areas where these ants have invaded, the numbers of *Mimetes* seedlings have dropped.

Seed Dormancy

Seed dormancy has two main functions: the first is synchronizing germination with the optimal conditions for survival of the resulting seedling; the second is spreading germination of a batch of seeds over time so that a catastrophe after germination (e.g. late frosts, drought, herbivory) does not result in the death of all offspring of a plant (bet-hedging). Seed dormancy is defined as a seed failing to germinate under environmental conditions optimal for germination, normally when the environment is at a suitable temperature with proper soil moisture. This true dormancy or innate dormancy is therefore caused by conditions within the seed that prevent germination. Thus dormancy is a state of the seed, not of the environment. Induced dormancy, enforced dormancy or seed quiescence occurs when a seed fails to germinate because the external environmental conditions are inappropriate for germination, mostly in response to conditions being too dark or light, too cold or hot, or too dry.

Seed dormancy is not the same as seed persistence in the soil or on the plant, though even in scientific publications dormancy and persistence are often confused or used as synonyms.

Often seed dormancy is divided into four major categories: exogenous; endogenous; combinational; and secondary. A more recent system distinguishes five classes of dormancy: morphological, physiological, morphophysiological, physical and combinational dormancy.

Exogenous dormancy is caused by conditions outside the embryo including:

- Physical dormancy or hard seed coats occurs when seeds are impermeable to water. At dormancy break a specialized structure, the 'water gap', is disrupted in response to environmental cues, especially temperature, so that water can enter the seed and germination can occur. Plant families where physical dormancy occurs include Anacardiaceae, Cannaceae, Convulvulaceae, Fabaceae and Malvaceae.
- Chemical dormancy considers species that lack physiological dormancy, but where a chemical prevents germination. This chemical can be leached out of the seed by rainwater or snow melt or be deactivated somehow. Leaching of chemical inhibitors from the seed

by rain water is often cited as an important cause of dormancy release in seeds of desert plants, however little evidence exists to support this claim.

Endogenous dormancy is caused by conditions within the embryo itself, including:

- **Morphological dormancy** where germination is prevented due to morphological characteristics of the embryo. In some species the embryo is just a mass of cells when seeds are dispersed, it is not differentiated. Before germination can take place both differentiation and growth of the embryo have to occur. In other species the embryo is differentiated but not fully grown (underdeveloped) at dispersal and embryo growth up to a species specific length is required before germination can occur. Examples of plant families where morphological dormancy occurs are Apiaceae, Cycadaceae, Liliaceae, Magnoliaceae and Ranunculaceae.
- **Morphophysiological dormancy** seeds with underdeveloped embryos, and which in addition have physiological components to dormancy. These seeds therefore require a dormancy-breaking treatments as well as a period of time to develop fully grown embryos. Plant families where morphophysiological dormancy occurs include Apiaceae, Aquifoliaceae, Liliaceae, Magnoliaceae, Papaveraceae and Ranunculaceae. Some plants with morphophysiological dormancy like Asarum or Trillium species have multiple types of dormancy, one affects radicle (root) growth while the other affects plumule (shoot) growth. The terms "double dormancy" and "2-year seeds" are used for species whose seeds need two years to complete germination or at least two winters and one summer. Dormancy of the radicle (seedling root)is broken during the first winter after dispersal while dormancy of the shoot bud is broken during the second winter.

- **Physiological dormancy** means that the embryo can, due to physiological causes, not generate enough power to break through the seed coat, endosperm or other covering structures. Dormancy is typically broken at cool wet, warm wet or warm dry conditions. Abscisic acid is usually the growth inhibitor in seeds and its production can be affected by light.
- **Drying**; some plants including a number of grasses and those from seasonally arid regions need a period of drying before they will germinate, the seeds are released but need to have a lower moisture content before germination can begin. If the seeds remain moist after dispersal, germination can be delayed for many months or even years. Many herbaceous plants from temperate climate zones have physiological dormancy that disappears with drying of the seeds. Other species will germinate after dispersal only under very narrow temperature ranges, but as the seeds dry they are able to germinate over a wider temperature range.
- **Combinational dormancy** In seeds with combinational dormancy the seed or fruit coat is impermeable to water and the embryo has physiological dormancy. Depending on the species physical dormancy can be broken before or after physiological dormancy is broken.
- **Secondary dormancy** is caused by conditions after the seed has been dispersed and occurs in some seeds when non-dormant seed is exposed to conditions that are not favorable to germination, very often high temperatures. The mechanisms of secondary dormancy are not yet fully understood but might involve the loss of sensitivity in receptors in the plasma membrane.

The following types of seed dormancy do not involve seed dormancy strictly spoken as lack of germination is prevented by the environment not by characteristics of the seed itself:

- **Photodormancy** or light sensitivity affects germination of some seeds. These photoblastic seeds need a period of darkness or light to germinate. In species with thin seed coats, light may be able to penetrate into the dormant embryo. The presence of light or the absence of light may trigger the germination process, inhibiting germination in some seeds buried too deeply or in others not buried in the soil.
- **Thermodormancy** is seed sensitivity to heat or cold. Some seeds including cocklebur and amaranth germinate only at high temperatures (30°C or 86°F) many plants that have seed that germinate in early to mid summer have thermodormancy and germinate only when the soil temperature is warm. Other seeds need cool soils to germinate, while others like celery are inhibited when soil temperatures are too warm. Often thermodormancy requirements disappear as the seed ages or dries.

Not all seeds undergo a period of dormancy. Seeds of some mangroves are viviparous, they begin to germinate while still attached to the parent. The large, heavy root allows the seed to penetrate into the ground when it falls. Many garden plants have seeds that will germinate readily as soon as they have water and are warm enough, though their wild ancestors may have had dormancy, these cultivated plants lack seed dormancy. After many generations of selective pressure by plant breeders and gardeners dormancy has been selected out.

For annuals, seeds are a way for the species to survive dry or cold seasons. Ephemeral plants are usually annuals that can go from seed to seed in as few as six weeks.

Seed Germination

Seed germination is a process by which a seed embryo develops into a seedling. It involves the reactivation of the metabolic pathways that lead to growth and the emergence of the radicle or seed root and plumule or shoot. The emergence of the seedling above the soil surface is the next phase of the plants growth and is called seedling establishment.

Three fundamental conditions must exist before germination can occur.

1. The embryo must be alive, called seed viability.
2. Any dormancy requirements that prevent germination must be overcome.
3. The proper environmental conditions must exist for germination.

Seed viability is the ability of the embryo to germinate and is affected by a number of different conditions. Some plants do not produce seeds that have functional complete embryos or the seed may have no embryo at all, often called empty seeds. Predators and pathogens can damage or kill the seed while it is still in the fruit or after it is dispersed. Environmental conditions like flooding or heat can kill the seed before or during germination. The age of the seed affects its health and germination ability: since the seed has a living embryo, over time cells die and cannot be replaced. Some seeds can live for a long time before germination, while others can only survive for a short period after dispersal before they die.

Seed vigour is a measure of the quality of seed, and involves the viability of the seed, the germination percentage, germination rate and the strength of the seedlings produced.

The germination percentage is simply the proportion of seeds that germinate from all seeds subject to the right conditions for growth. The germination rate is the length of time it takes for the seeds to germinate. Germination percentages and rates are affected by seed viability, dormancy and environmental effects that impact on the seed and seedling. In agriculture and horticulture quality seeds have high viability, measured by germination percentage plus the rate of germination. This is given as a per cent of germination over a certain amount of time, 90 per cent germination in 20 days, for example. 'Dormancy' is covered above; many plants produce seeds with varying degrees of dormancy, and different seeds from the same fruit can have different degrees of dormancy. It's possible to have seeds with no dormancy if they are dispersed right away and do not dry (if the seeds dry they go into physiological dormancy). There is great variation amongst plants and a dormant seed is still a viable seed even though the germination rate might be very low.

Environmental conditions effecting seed germination include; water, oxygen, temperature and light.

Three distinct phases of seed germination occur:

1. water imbibition;
2. lag phase; and
3. radicle emergence.

In order for the seed coat to split, the embryo must imbibe (soak up water), which causes it to swell, splitting the seed coat. However, the nature of the seed coat determines how rapidly water can penetrate and subsequently initiate germination. The rate of imbibition is dependent on the permeability of the seed coat, amount of water in the environment and the area of contact the seed has to the source of water. For some seeds, imbibing too much water too quickly can kill the seed. For some seeds, once water is imbibed the germination process cannot be stopped, and drying then becomes fatal. Other seeds can imbibe and lose water a few times without causing ill effects, but drying can cause secondary dormancy.

Inducing Germination

Scarification which allows water and gases to penetrate into the seed, include methods that physically break the hard seed coats or soften them by chemicals. Means of scarification include soaking in hot water or poking holes in the seed with a pin or rubbing them on sandpaper or cracking with a press or hammer. Soaking the seeds in solvents or acids is also effective for many seeds. Sometimes fruits are harvested while the seeds are still immature and the seed coat is not fully developed and sown right away before the seed coat become impermeable. Under natural conditions seed coats are worn down by rodents chewing on the seed, the seeds rubbing against rocks (seeds are moved by the wind or water currents), by undergoing freezing and thawing of surface water, or passing through an animal's digestive tract. In the latter case, the seed coat protects the seed from digestion, while often weakening the seed coat such that the embryo is ready to sprout when it gets deposited (along with a bit of fertilizer) far from the parent plant. Microorganisms are often effective in breaking down hard seed coats and are sometimes used by people as a treatment, the seeds are stored in a moist warm sandy medium for several months under non-sterile conditions.

Stratification also called moist-chilling is a method to break down physiological dormancy and involves the addition of moisture to the seeds so they imbibe water and then the seeds are subject to a period of moist chilling to after-ripen the embryo. Sowing outside in late summer and fall and allowing to overwinter outside under cool conditions is an effective way to stratify seeds, some seeds respond more favourably to periods of oscillating temperatures which are part of the natural environment.

Leaching or the soaking in water removes chemical inhibitors in some seeds that prevent germination. Rain and melting snow naturally accomplish this task. For seeds planted in gardens, running water is best - if soaked in a container, 12 to 24 hours of soaking is sufficient. Soaking longer, especially in stagnant water that is not changed, can result in oxygen starvation and seed death. Seeds with hard seed coats can be soaked in hot water to break open the impermeable cell layers that prevent water intake.

Other methods used to assist in the germination of seeds that have dormancy include prechilling, predrying, daily alternation of temperature, light exposure, potassium nitrate, the use of plant growth regulators like gibberellins, cytokinins, ethylene, thiourea, sodium hypochlorite plus others. Some seeds germinate best after a fire, for some seeds fire cracks hard seed coats while in other seeds chemical dormancy is broken in reaction to the presence of smoke, liquid smoke is often used by gardeners to assist in the germination of these species.

The origin of seed plants is a problem that still remains unsolved. However, more and more data tends to place this origin in the middle Devonian. The description in 2004 of the proto-seed *Runcaria heinzelinii* in the Givetian of Belgium is an indication of that ancient origin of seed-plants. As with modern ferns, most land plants before this time reproduced by sending spores into the air, that would land and become whole new plants.

The first "true" seeds are described from the upper Devonian, which is probably the theater of their true first evolutionary radiation. The seed plants progressively became one of the major elements of nearly all ecosystems.

Many seeds are edible and the majority of human calories comes from seeds , especially from cereals, legumes and nuts. Seeds also provide most cooking oils, many beverages and spices and some important food additives. In different seeds the seed embryo or the endosperm dominates and provides most of the nutrients. The storage proteins of the embryo and endosperm differ in their amino acid content and physical properties. For example the gluten of wheat, important in providing the elastic property to bread dough is strictly an endosperm protein.

Seeds are used to propagate many crops such as cereals, legumes, forest trees, turfgrasses and pasture grasses. Particularly in developing countries, a major constraint faced is the inadequacy of the marketing channels to get the seed to poor farmers. Thus the use of farmer-retained seed remains quite common.

Poison and Food Safety

While some seeds are edible, others are harmful, poisonous or deadly. Plants and seeds often contain chemical compounds to discourage herbivores and seed predators. In some cases, these compounds simply taste bad (such as in mustard), but other compounds are toxic or break down into toxic compounds within the digestive system. Children, being smaller than adults, are more susceptible to poisoning by plants and seeds.

A deadly poison, ricin, comes from seeds of the castor bean. Reported lethal doses are anywhere from two to eight seeds, though only a few deaths have been reported when castor beans have been ingested by animals.

In addition, seeds containing amygdalin—apple, apricot, bitter almond, peach, plum, cherry, quince, and others—when consumed in sufficient amounts, may cause Cyanide poisoning. Other seeds that contain poisons include annona, cotton, custard apple, datura, uncooked durian, golden chain, horse-chestnut, larkspur, locoweed, lychee, nectarine, rambutan, rosary pea, sour sop, sugar apple, wisteria, and yew. The seeds of the strychnine tree are also poisonous, containing the poison strychnine.

The seeds of many legumes, including the common bean (*Phaseolus vulgaris*), contain proteins called lectins which can cause gastric distress if the beans are eaten without cooking. The common bean and many others, including the soybean, also contain trypsin inhibitors which interfere with the action of the digestive enzyme trypsin. Normal cooking processes degrade lectins and trypsin inhibitors to harmless forms.

List of Edible Seeds

A list of edible seeds here includes seeds that are directly foodstuffs, rather than yielding derived products.

A variety of species can provide edible seeds. Of the six major plant parts, seeds are the most important source of human food. The other five major plant parts are roots, stems, leaves, flowers, and fruits. Most edible seeds are angiosperms, but a few are gymnosperms. The most important seed food source is cereals, followed by legumes, and nuts.

The list is divided into the following categories:

- Beans (or Legumes) are protein-rich soft seeds.
- Cereals (or grains) are grass-like crops that are harvested for their dry seeds. These seeds are often ground to make flour. Cereals provide almost half of all calories consumed in the world. Botanically, true cereals are members of the Poaceae or Grass family.
- Pseudocereals are cereal crops that are not members of the Poaceae or Grass Family.
- Nuts are botanically a specific type of fruit but the term is also applied to many edible seeds that are not botanically nuts.
- Gymnosperms produce nut-like seeds but not flowers or fruits.

Beans, also known as legumes or pulses include:

- Lentils have been part of the human diet since the Neolithic period
- Chickpeas
- Cowpeas
- Dry beans

  Common bean
- Several species of Vigna, such as the lentil
- Fava or broad beans
- Hyacinth bean
- Lablab
- Lentils
- Lupins
- Moringa oleifera
- Peas

- Peanuts
- Pigeon peas
- Sterculia
- Velvet beans
- Winged beans
- Yam beans
- Soybeans

Although some beans can be consumed raw, some need to be heated before consumption. In certain cultures, beans that needed heating anyhow were immediatelly prepared as a seed cake. Some beans that needed heating include:

- *Acacia* spp. (e.g. *Acacia aneura* (mulga), *Acacia cowleana*, *Acacia estrophiolata* (ironweed), *Acacia ligulata* (umbrella bush), *Acacia murrayana* (tjuntjula), *Acacia tetragonophylla* (wakalpulka), *Acacia kempeana* (Witchetty bush), *Acacia coriacea* (Wiry wattle), *Acacia notabilis*, *Acacia pyrifolia*, *Acacia tetragonophylla*, *Acacia victoriae*, *Acacia sophorae*, *Acacia stenophylla*, *Acacia tumida*)
- *Aleurites moluccana*
- *Atriplex nummularia* (Old man saltbush)
- *Panicum* spp. (e.g. *Panicum australiense*, *Panicum decompositum*, *Panicum effusum*)
- *Amaranthus mitchellii*
- *Amaranthus grandiflorus*
- *Brachiaria* spp. (e.g. *Brachiaria piligera Brachiaria milliformis*)
- *Brachychiton* spp. (e.g. *Brachychiton diversifolium Brachychiton gregorii*, *Brachychiton paradoxum*, *Brachychiton populneum*)
- *Bruguiera rheedii*
- *Calandrinia balonensis*
- *Canarium australianum*

- *Canavalia maritima*
- *Entada phaseolides*
- *Eragrostris* spp. (Wangunu) (e.g. *Eragrostris eriopoda*)
- *Eucalyptus leptopoda*
- *Eucalyptus microtheca*
- *Astrelba pectinata* (Mitchell grass)
- *Portulaca oleracea*
- *Portulaca intraterranea*
- *Marsilea drummondii* (Nardoo)
- *Nymphae gigantea*
- *Rhyncharrhena linearis*
- *Themeda australis*

True cereals are the seeds of certain species of grass. Three – maize, wheat and rice – account for about half of the calories consumed by people every year. Grains can be ground to make flour, used as the basis of bread, cake, noodles or other food products. They can also be boiled or steamed, either whole or ground, and eaten as is. Many cereals are present or past staple foods, provided a large fraction of the calories in the places that they are eaten. Cereals include:

- Barley
- Fonio
- Maize (corn)
- Pearl Millet
- Oats
- Palmer's grass
- Rice
- Rye
- Sorghum
- Spelt
- Teff
- Triticale

- Wheat
- Wild rice
- Pseudocereals

Quinoa is not a grass, but its seeds have been eaten for 6000 years.

- Breadnut
- Buckwheat
- Cattail
- Chia
- Flax
- Grain amaranth
- Kañiwa
- Pitseed Goosefoot
- Quinoa
- Wattleseed (also called *acacia seed*)

According to the botanical definition, nuts are a particular kind of seed. Chestnuts, hazelnuts, and acorns are examples of nuts, under this definition. In culinary terms, however, the term is used more broadly to include fruits that are not botanically qualified as nuts, but that have a similar appearance and culinary role. Examples of culinary nuts include almonds, peanuts and cashews.

- Almond
- Beech
- Brazil nut
- Candlenut
- Cashew
- Chestnuts, including:
- Chinese Chestnut
- Sweet Chestnut
- Colocynth
- *Cucurbita ficifolia*

- Filbert
- *Gevuina avellana*
- Hickory, including
- Pecan
- Shagbark Hickory
- *Terminalia catappa*
- Hazelnut
- Indian Beech
- Kola nut
- Macadamia
- Malabar chestnut
- Pistacia
- Mamoncillo
- Maya nut
- Mongongo
- Oak acorns
- Ogbono nut
- Paradise nut
- Pili nut
- Walnut
- Water Caltrop

Nut-like Gymnosperm Seeds

Pine nuts are Gymnosperm seeds that are edible.

- Cycads
- Ginkgo
- *Gnetum gnemon*
- Juniper
- Monkey-puzzle
- Pine nuts, including
- Chilgoza Pine
- Korean Pine

- Stone Pine
- Colorado Pinyon
- Mexican Pinyon
- Single-leaf Pinyon
- Podocarps

Cempedak Egusi Euryale ferox (Fox nut) Fluted pumpkin Hemp seed Jackfruit Lotus seed Malabar gourd Pumpkin seed Sunflower seed.

3 Importance of Seeds in Agriculture

Seed is a fundamental input for agriculture. Indeed, seed is the single most important input in all crop-based farming systems and a prerequisite for most of the world's food production. More than being the basis of production for the majority of the world's crops, seed determines the upper limit on yield and therefore on the ultimate productivity of all other inputs.

Crop genetic diversity is the basis for research and improvement of crop varieties.

Access to a wide range of genetic diversity allows farmers and plant breeders to adapt a crop to heterogeneous and changing environments, developing cultivars with high levels of adaptation to biotic and abiotic stresses and to human preferences. This makes the conservation of genetic resources important in addressing future challenges of research and crop improvement, seeking to intensify agricultural production and increase food supply, and trying to respond to farmers' different requirements and preferences.

In the 1960s the introduction of science based agricultural technologies often combined with governmental subsidies, increased the productivity of agriculture and this became known as the green revolution. What is less known is that for the last forty years this rapid increase of productivity has largely been sustained in the developing countries. Most of these gains have been in Asia and Latin America. However, according to researchers there is recent evidence that impacts of varietal improvement in rice, maizecassava and other crops have now started to show in Sub-Saharan Africa.

In the early green revolution period around 20 per cent of the increase in agricultural production was simply due to an expansion of the area cultivated, and other parts can be attributed to improved agricultural practices and increased use of inputs such as fertilizer and insecticides.

However, for all developing countries some 21 per cent of the growth in yield and about 17 per cent of production growth could be attributed alone to the use of improved seed. Securing the conservation of crop genetic resources and farmers' access to seed of the desired varieties and of good quality is therefore a very important management issue for farmers and a concern for society in order to achieve food security.

Informal Seed

Informal seed systems are central to conserving crop genetic diversity, sustaining farmers' livelihoods and food security, and making small-scale agriculture a productive and viable option. Several authors have pointed out that informal seed systems are mostly based on traditional social alliances and family relations, cast in the context of mutual interdependence and trust, often forming dynamic networks with a high degree of complexity. Still, although many authors have emphasized the role of informal seed exchange for the conservation of crop genetic diversity as well as for the improvement of farmers' seed security, little attention has been given to the detailed study of the mechanisms of informal seed systems, and relatively little is known about the factors and processes that influence and shape small-scale farmers' practices with regards to informal seed exchange. As stated by researchers: "The flow of seeds or farmer-to-farmer exchange of seed is a neglected area of research. There is an urgent need to understand more in detail the process of farmer-to-farmer exchange of seed".

A better understanding of the dynamics of local seed management can contribute to several important areas related to the improvement of supply of quality seed for agricultural production in poor countries, as well as to the conservation of crop genetic diversity in farmers' fields. These include: Better targeting of agricultural research and crop improvement towards the needs and priorities of poor farmers in the developing world:

- Faster and more widespread introduction of improved material by linking the formal and informal sector more effectively;
- Fostering new joint approaches to crop improvement where thecontributions of farmer management is integrated deliberately into the improvement process;
- Assessment of the potentials and problems of *in situ* germplasm conservation.

In most developing countries two different systems of plant genetic resources management have developed. One is an informal plant genetic resource management system based on farmers' local knowledge. The other is a formal, science-based plant genetic resource management system consisting of institutions for plant conservation, breeding and seed multiplication and distribution. In many cases the formal sector evolved as a result of the emphasis in the 1970s and 1980s on formal crop genetic resource management, the science-based approach of the green revolution and the ideas on modernization of agricultural production.

The informal and formal genetic resource management systems are, however, interlinked and the informal sector may for example supply seed derived directly from germplasm from the formal sector (i.e. improved material).

A distinction can be made between seed supplied directly from the formal or the informal sector, and furthermore a distinction can be made between improved material, and land races or creolized material. The latter is a mixture of one or more landraces with improved material or simply improved material that has been cultivated on farm for a number of cropping cycles. In practice it is difficult to distinguish land races from creolized material, and theterm land race will be used to cover farmer produced material without trying to determine if it contains elements of improved material. Seed provided from the formal sector is generally improved seed, but seed from the informal sector can be anywhere on the sliding scale from improved material to creolized and to land races. The use of the term 'improved' when referring to seed from the formal sector is a question of using conventional terminology and does not imply that land races have not been improved by farmers' management.

In developed countries the formal sector is the dominant system for seed supply, crop development and conservation of crop genetic resources. Most crop production in these countries depends on seed of modern varieties provided by the formal seed sector. In many cases the informal seed sector has almost disappeared or serves only hobby-farmers, though in some cases, according to some authors the informal seed sector continues to play a significant role. For example it is reported by researchers, that only 50 per cent of the total seed demand of overall agricultural crops in Germany is supplied by the formal seed sector, and that in Spain it is as low as 10 per cent, while the same data for Denmark, and the Netherlands and are reported to be 95 and 75 per cent respectively. It should, however, be kept in mind that the apparently low use of the formal sector as seed supplier does not mean that the material is not improved material.

Researcher estimates that around three quarters of the world's farmers use farm-saved seed, and unlike farmers in developed countries or commercial farmers in developing countries, small-scale farmers in the developing world, who produce primarily for their own consumption, often depend almost entirely on themselves or other farmers for seed. In many developing countries, therefore, informal seed sources supply the vast majority of the seed. Within this broad field a number of authors have set out to describe local seed systems and their importance in relation to agricultural production, among others researchers. These and other studies have stressed the importance of informal seed supply in terms of seed security for small-scale farmers in developing countries, for example in years of deficit harvest or in emergency situations.

Although the adoption of improved varieties for a number of food crops in developing countries is significant, the share of the formal sector in the total seed supply remains low. Furthermore, a considerable part of the spread of improved materials has taken place through the informal seed sector, for example as farmer-to-farmer distribution of seed of improved and creolized varieties.

The mechanisms of local seed exchange have important implications in several respects. It is essential for individual farmers to be able to obtain seed of a certain variety and quality in order to secure agricultural production and food supply. However it also has implications of utmost importance in relation to the evolution and conservation of crop genetic diversity.

The literature on seed systems research is diverse and reflects very different approaches to the subject matter. Rather than presenting a disciplinary overview of the literature, it is described from a thematic angle, following three main approaches, namely, the development approach, the biodiversity conservationist approach, and the emergency seed relief approach. The presentation does not focus narrowly on seed, but sees it in the larger context of agricultural development and agricultural research.

Modernisation of Agriculture and the Green Revolution

The re-discovery in the beginning of the 20th century of Gregor Mendel's findings regarding the genetics of plant reproduction triggered the development of modern plant breeding. The advances in plant breeding and other technologies, and their impacts in terms of crop yields, paved the way for formal crop improvement and seed production. Large investments were made in agricultural research.

Increasingly specialized organisations developed in the form of a formal seed sector, composed of specialized public and private enterprises involved in plant breeding, seed production and distribution, and served by a system of legislative standards for seed quality and variety protection. This also brought substantial changes in the role of farmers in crop improvement and conservation of crop genetic resources.

In parallel to plant breeding, the mechanization of agriculture was also fast increasing, and chemical fertilizers and eventually chemical pesticides were developed. The success of science and technology in agricultural modernization in The United States and Europe after the Second World War became a model for development in the third world. Several years of severe food crisis and famine in various parts of the world, in particular in South Asia, led to the initiation of the development of modern crop varieties for developing countries in the 1950s. The success of the efforts, also known as '*the green evolution*', to increase yields were indisputable and over the ollowing decades world grain production more than doubled due to the spread of new agricultural technologies, in particular modern high-yielding crop varieties and new agricultural practices In view of the initial successes of the green revolution, agricultural development agencies and governments in developing countries sought to stimulate the flow of seed of modern varieties to farmers. In many developing countries, formal sectors for plant breeding, seed production and distribution programmes were established, often with support from international donor agencies, and with public agencies carrying out most of the activities. For the most part, these systems for plant genetic resource management were modelled on the formal seed sectors in industrialized countries, and activities were professionalized and segregated.

In development circles, technology came to be seen as the generator of development and growth. Technology became the point of departure, and the transfer of technology became the dominant approach towards development. The 'ideology of the neutrality of technology' gained currency. According to the latter, any adverse impacts on poor farmers should not be blamed on the inherent nature of the technology but rather on the agrarian structure, the economic policy environment or the agro-ecological conditions under which the technologies are implemented. As researcher comment, instead of striving for crops and cropping systems to be finely in tune with their environment through natural balance, environments were increasingly adapted to the requirements of the crops.

Research station technologies were viewed as superior to farmer practices since crops performed better on-station with standardized inputs. The failure of modern varieties to spread into marginal areas was thought to be rooted in the conservatism and backwardness of traditional farmers. New and superior technologies were envisioned to be adopted first by a few, more progressive farmers, in order to subsequently filter down to the smaller, more traditional farmers, as they realised the benefits gained by the early adopters.

Technological and economical determinist approaches to technology diffusion assume that a technology will spread almost by itself if it is technologically superior to, or more profitable than, existing technologies. However, experience has shown that though these factors are important, they are by no means a guarantee for success. Most technologies that fulfil these criteria have no or very little practical impact, and often it can be observedthat the technology that achieves widespread adoption is not the best from a technological stand point, nor necessarily the most profitable. Modern approaches to technology diffusion stress the importance of conceptualising technology diffusion as a social process, where people's perceptions and networks play a crucial role. In addition, when the technologies are aimed at resource poor people, experience also highlights the importance of involving the people early in the process in order to adapt the development to their particular situation.

The Challenge of Reaching Farmers in Marginal Areas

Some have argued that international agricultural research is organized in a way which creates structures that are frequently indifferent and insensitive to the needs of small farmers. Another way of putting this could be that the focus of international agricultural research organisations on the production of global public goods, such as generally applicable technologies, has not been able to sufficiently address more local needs or preferences.

The Green Revolution technologies were particularly successful in favourable environments which were adequate for the improved germplasm that was available at that time. In particular this was the case in the irrigated areas in Asia and in Latin America. The improved germplasm available at the beginning of the green revolution was not well adapted to the production conditions, for example, in large parts of Africa.

This limitation was further aggravated by the fact that when artificial fertilizer is applied, cereal landraces often grow too tall and lodge. In many cases this meant that unless improved germplasm was used, farmers could not use chemical fertilizer to increase productivity in their landraces. In less favourable and marginal areas, where production conditions are usually more complex and more risk prone, the green revolution and the formal seed sector have generally had considerably less success. Low soil fertility, frequently occurring droughts, inundations or other climatic hazards reduce the productivity of the crop.

Likewise, access to agricultural inputs like capital, land, labour, water, and fertilizer, is generally limited, more expensive, and more variable due to bad roads and remote markets. In these conditions farmers may lack cash to buy seed. In addition, higher seed quality may not be expressed in higher yields because of other limiting factors, and the purchase of expensive seed may not be considered economical.

Farmers in these areas may grow a wider range of locally adapted varieties with different characteristics. Varieties that are suitable for favourable high-input conditions may not prove the best option for low-input conditions in these marginal areas. Moreover, modern varieties that are bred for high yield may not serve the many different purposes for which a subsistence farmer produces a crop, such as special preferences for home consumption as well as the need for secondary products. Farmers in marginal areas often have different needs and require varieties with multiple characteristics in particular combinations. This can be difficult to address through formal seed programmes.

Many developing country governments and international development agencies have until recently only supported formal sector institutions forplant genetic resources, and have linked credit, subsidies, research and extension to the adoption of modern varieties. The introduction of Structural Adjustment Programmes in the 1990s reduced, or in many cases completely reintroduction moved, the subsidies for this kind of agriculture and has probably increasedthe number of farmers unable to take advantage of modern crop improvement.

Furthermore, in several countries public sector programmes have faced a series of problems, including severe lack of resources, and as a result they have often produced less than expected. At the same time private sector seed enterprises have encountered high transaction costs and inappropriate legislatory frameworks. In many regards, NGOs have therefore been seen as an important complement and go-between for the strengthening of linkages between the formal seed sector and farmers.

However, not all NGOs have been equally successful in this role. Researchers report on a review of 19 NGOs involved in local seed production and distribution. Though also acknowledging several strengths of NGOs, the authors note that operations are generally small-scale and depend heavily on external funding. Furthermore, in severalcases they lack technical expertise, and rather than being innovative, activities appear often to be moulded after those of the formal seed sector.

The diminishing support from governments for farmers is further aggravated by the increased use of intellectual property rights related to crop improvement. Previously a lot of agricultural research was done in public research institutions and there was a relatively free flow of new technologies, but with the advent of biotechnology, new discoveries are more frequently protected by intellectual property rights and the improvements in productivity are likely to take even longer to reach small scale farmers in developingcountries.

The importance of seed regulations and legislatory frameworks in relation to efforts to support and strengthen farmers' access to seed of diverse varieties is increasingly being acknowledged, and attention to these aspects has grown significantly. Meanwhile, other approaches have emerged which focus more on the facilitation of farmers' access to seed within local contexts, for example, 'seed vouchers and fairs'.

Advances in agricultural productivity have not only benefited farmers. The prices of agricultural products have fallen over the last decades, and consumers are the largest beneficiaries of the production increase. Some smallscale farmers, particularly in less favourable agro-ecological regions, whowere not able to increase their productivity sufficiently to compensate for falling prices may in fact be worse off today. In summary, therefore, the science-driven increase in agricultural productivity has hugely benefitd consumers, and also benefited the farmers who have the capacity to increase their productivity. However, effectively reaching farmers in more marginal and more remote areas remains a challenge.

Since the beginning of agriculture farmers have domesticated and developed crops, adapting them to diverse environments and specific human preferences through thousands of years of selection and experimentation. Farmers' crop improvement experimentation, as well as the management, production and exchange of crop genetic resources by and amongst farmers are often referred to as informal seed systems, local seed systems or farmers' seed systems. In these, crop improvement, seed supply and conservation perspectives are combined at the local level in farmers' strategies for local crop development. The adaptation and improvement of varieties, seed production, utilization and exchange, as well as the conservation of crop genetic resources, are all integrated activities in these systems.

They are part of the local agricultural system and are usually carried out on the same farm through processes that are based on local knowledge accumulated and used in the community through generations.

The point of departure for this approach is the focus on seed as an important source of germplasm and its role in small-scale agriculture as well as in the evolution of crop genetic diversity and in crop improvement initiatives.

During the last decades concerns about the loss of biodiversity have increased substantially and *genetic erosion* has become a much debated issue, particularly since a diverse set of genetically variable crop landraces has been replaced by a few, genetically uniform, high-yielding varieties.

The increasing pressure on land and labour increases the importance of yield as a selection criterion for farmers, leading to intensified crop production, the adoption of improved varieties with higher yield potentials, the use of more inputs, and the planting of fewer varieties on the farm. Fading cultural diversity and traditions have also been associated with the increasing disappearanceof local cultivars.

Concerns about the loss of plant genetic resources are especially valid in areas of crop domestication, where diversity is concentrated and where farmers maintain not only seed of local varieties of ancestral crop populations but also the human knowledge and behavioural practices that have shaped this diversity for generations.

In many regions local cultivars tend to be left to the more marginal, riskprone habitats and ethnological niches for which the improved varieties are less suitable. Though traditional varieties tend to be sturdier, the tendency to focus their use on marginal lands increases the risk of losing some of these varieties in a bad year.

Some argue that low input farming systems may be particularly subject to genetic vulnerability because of pests and tropical conditions, weak infrastructure and economic marginality. Anthropologists and others have argued that crop genetic diversity is one of the principal means that farmers in low input farming systems use in order to protect production, for example planting several varieties of the same crop as a way of confronting risks and heterogeneous production conditions. From this perspective the loss of crop genetic diversity may therefore leave local cultivators even more vulnerable.

From a social interactionist perspective, local technical knowledge, skills and capacities to manage plant genetic resources are embedded in the cultural, ecological and sociological context of the community. Farmers' local experimentations are not based on scientific theoretical models, but emerge from strong interests in and knowledge of practical local application that provide options for improving their livelihoods.

Modern theories on knowledge argue that science and technology are socially constructed and embody social relations. The development and uptake of scientific and technological knowledge rely upon and modify existing modes of communication and organisational relations. It is by no means a passive process. Rather, it must be considered an active process, an interaction between various agents within particular cultural and organisational contexts, during which the technology may be adapted and transformed, influenced by a series of social and cultural factors.

Local institutions for managing plant genetic resources only seldom take the shape of organisations. They commonly consist of shared norms and practices within a community or ethnic group of people. While the natural resource management by local institutions is often associated with conflict over access and use, plant genetic resources are renewable and are therefore seldom the cause of conflict over access at the local level. Plant genetic resource management is largely the product of social processes and institutions in the community. When these change it is likely also to have an effect on local plant genetic resource management.

In general, studies investigating these aspects at the local level have often portrayed small-scale farmers as the caretakers of important crop genetic resources who continue to maintain and cultivate diverse varieties. However, most small-scale farmers do not maintain crop genetic resources merely for the sake of conservation. Rather, it appears that many farmers give social value to local resources and make special use of diverse crop varieties, either for consumption purposes or as a means of confronting heterogeneous agricultural conditions.

Similarly, the ability of local seed management practices to adapt varieties to specific cultural, economic and social requirements through the application of farmers' knowledge and skills has been documented. In many cases decisions regarding varietal choice depend on multiple considerations, not just on yield. As researchers point out, such issues can be illuminated by in-depth, qualitative studies.

Seed Relief Approach

The seed relief approach grew out of efforts to address seed security in connection to disaster or emergency contexts.

Obviously inspiration was found in food relief programmes in such situations, with the idea that seed relief would contribute to the restoration of local food production.

Originally seed relief interventions were based on the assumption that no seed were available in the affected region. The response was therefore to bring in large quantities of seed of the most important crops and simply distribute it. Later it was found that in fact, the assumption that the problem was one of seed availability was not always correct. Studies showed that often local seed systems were quite resilient, even under very extreme circumstances.

In some emergency situations (e.g. the civil war in Rwanda) bean seed was in fact available in the local seed system, and some farmers managed to plant and harvest in spite of the war and its devastating effects on society. These revelations showed that farmers' problems acquiring seed during crisis were not necessarily due to lack of seed availability. Instead, it seems that farmers' problems in many cases stem from difficulties of access, because the crisis has destroyed social networks (as in the case of Rwanda), thereby disrupting the customary channels for informal seed acquisitions, or because farmers simply lack the means with which to acquire the seed, for example through purchase or barter.

A new 'paradigm' for seed aid interventions has therefore emerged, shifting the focus from merely concentrating on direct seed aid distribution, to a broader approach more oriented towards agricultural rehabilitation and development Acute stress normally refers to a sudden and very violent form of crisis which affects large numbers of people in large areas, such as natural disasters or war. Chronic stress, on the other hand, refers to a constant situation of vulnerability and crisis, for example, very difficult agro-ecological and/or socioeconomic conitions. Chronic stress is closely linked to severe poverty and may not affect all groups equally.

Seed relief in the form of direct distribution of seed brought in from elsewhere has been criticized in a number of other respects. Repeated relief interventions in the same area have turned out often to be due to a misinterpretation of the situation, that is, where a case of chronic stress has been interpreted as an acute stress. In some cases, such repeated emergency seed interventions have led to seed aid dependency and the destruction of local seed systems.

Seed relief interventions have also been criticized for not always presenting appropriate crops or varieties and for not leaving farmers sufficient choice. In some cases it has even been criticized as an unfair or 'back-door' method for promoting modern varieties. Similarly the introduction of large quantities of seed from elsewhere, for example of modern crop varicties, has been associated with risks for local crop genetic diversity, and finally, seed relief interventions have been seen as inappropriately benefiting certain actors from the formal sector, for instance by providing opportunities for corruption.

The direct seed distribution approach is also sometimes called the seeds and tools approach. It has been criticized in a number of regards: for not always being based on, for example, a proper assessment of the problem (e.g. availability vs. accessibility), which in turn can result in aid dependency; for being based on a negative perception of farmer seed systems; and for benefiting other sectors more than the intended farmers, such as the formal, commercial sector, or the use of inappropriate distribution channels.

As an alternative to the Seeds and Tools approach, agricultural rehabilitation and development tends towards interventions that strengthen existing seed systems and with that the linkages between the formal and informal seed sectors. New strategies emphasize working to understand and strengthen local seed systems, and on integrating relief and development approaches in seed interventions. Rather than focusing solely on direct seed distribution, interventions now try to place grater emphasis on strengthening seed systems from the inside.

Local Knowledge

The various ideas and practices that form part of farmers' seed management can be considered a form of local knowledge – a central concern of many anthropological studies. However, knowledge is also an important field of theory and study in itself, where elements from many disciplines including philosophy, psychology, and anthropology can play a role. Approaches within theory on knowledge can tentatively be divided into two; those that focus mainly on social aspects as distinct from those that relate to cognitive aspects.

The former have focused on issues related to power, how power influences what is considered knowledge, and how discourses on knowledge reproduce power relations. Another important contribution has been the recognition that knowledge is not unitary and systematized, either for the individual, or for the social group; on the contrary, knowledge is fragmentary, diffuse, and multi-layered. Considerations of power and interface are central to many studies involving local people's negotiations with government officials or representatives of private companies. Certain schools of anthropology have, in particular, stressed the usefulness of cognitive theories of knowledge. This has been convincingly argued by researchers who underline the limitations of relyingon overly linguistic models of knowledge.

This and other analytical aspects of local knowledge, in particular the communication and negotiation of local understandings, and some of the analytical and methodological implications these imply. This is followed by a presentation and discussion of several aspects of local seed concepts and practices in the study area.

Collective Action

As an analytical concept, collective action has been particularly useful in the study of social movements and the management by multiple actors of public goods or common resources such as forests, fisheries, rangelands, irrigation.

However, though crop genetic resources are broadly regarded as a public good, they are very different from other natural resource public goods for which the main problem is over-use. The case of crop genetic resources is quite the opposite - in fact, for many landraces and wild relatives, their conservation is often entirely dependent on their continued use and from a conservation point of view, one might say, theore they are used the better.

Most definitions of collective action share the notion that it necessarily involves multiple actors and is directed towards the achievement of certain conceptual framework and methodological strategy common interests or goals. While the definition of what constitutes the collective, and to what degree the actions it takes can be said to represent a common purpose, remain highly debated, a large body of research has documented the processes by which collective organisation emerges and constitutes itself. This literature gives attention to the rise and functioning of both formal and informal organisations. Moreover, close attention has been paid tohow collectivities have developed that concern themselves with sets of rights and responsibilities related to the use of common resources.

On a more theoretical level, the study of collective action is marked by a divide between those who are interested in social movements as distinct sociocultural entities with a common identity, and those who take their point of departure as the lived experiences and agency of multiple social actors who negotiate to form coalitions that are continuously being reshaped.

Social Embeddedness

Farmer seed transactions can be regarded as an economic practice, involving the exchange of a good between two parties. Rational choice theory has played an important role in the development of economic theory and in several respects has contributed greatly to the understanding of economic phenomena.

However, with regard to the study of the practices of economic actors at a more specific level, various critics have pointed to the limitations of theories based on utility maximization. In particular the critique has been directed at the view of actors as independent, 'atomized' and 'rational' decisionmakers with little or no concern for the role of human emotions, social interaction and networks.

Seed transactions can be looked at from a market perspective. In much economic theory a competitive market is viewed as being constituted by a large number of consumers and suppliers who do not influence market dynamics individually. Furthermore, it is often assumed that the actors have perfect information, and that social relations do not significantly influence actors in their transactions. Yet, many detailed studies of social behaviour in real market situations seriously question these assumptions. For example, distances himself from the utilitarian theories of classical and neo-classical economics, and discards the idea of economic behaviour as something heavily embedded in pre-market societies which unfolds and becomes moreautonomous as modernization occurs. As an alternative, he proposes a more integrated view of human actors capable of processing information and experience and acting upon it, but who do not exist independently of the social context of which they form a part.

From an analytical point of view, farmers' seed exchanges can be regarded as interactions in which social capital is mobilized. The concept of social capital has been much debated and used in many different ways to deal with the social aspects of economic practice. Researcher defines social capital as different forms or institutions of social organisation that allow individuals to coordinate and pursue interests for their mutual benefit. He furthermore posits a clear relation between the amount of social capital and the level of economic development and democracy in any given society.

While the work has played an important role in popularising the concept of social capital and has been widely used, among others by the World Bank, it has also been criticized by many for being misleading and for obscuring the role of power.

Social capital has also been described as the result of institutional and individual or collective investments in the reproduction of social relationships that are directly usable in the short or long term. According to researcher, social capital is constantly reproduced through a process in which goods, favours, information, etc. are continuously exchanged as a means of recognizing and affirming social relations and group membership.

Others distinguish between different meanings of social capital according to their origin and types of trust. According to researchers, social capital can be seen, on one hand, as "a 'stock' of trust and an emotional attachment to a group or society at large that facilitate the provision of public goods"; they call this generalized trust. On the other hand, social capital can also take the form of "an individual asset that benefits a single individual or firm", which they refer to as personalized trust.

Other uses of the term merely signal awareness of the significance of social aspects in relation to economic or political processes, without actually contributing to an improved understanding of the issues in question. A related view is that social capital is no more than resources that are obtained through social relations and networks. Another interpretation is that social capital must be understood as the ability of actors to use social networks in order to mobilize resources, and not as the actual resources themselves. Furthermore social capital is often viewed as an asset and in some regards also a constraint. Farmers mobilize social networks in order to negotiate favourable terms for seed transactions and to acquire maize seed with favoured characteristics.

Trust

As a good, seed lacks transparency. That is, the person acquiring the seed cannot know the characteristics of the plant the seed may produce merely by looking at it, and therefore must rely on the information provided by the seed supplier. This makes trust an important issue in seed transactions.

Trust is relationally and culturally constructed. The notion of trust is often used to describe the expectation or confidence one has that someone will act in a particular way, for example with honesty or sincerity. Different categories of trust have been discussed and it has also been pointed out that, while trust is generally regarded as something positive and desirable, it can, under certain circumstances, also be regarded as something negative, depending on one's interpretation of the context.

With regard to transaction and social exchange it has been noted that the cultivation and use of trust and trust relations tends to grow in importance under different conditions of risk and uncertainty. Thus, the notion of trust appears to be able to contribute to a feeling of security, when social actors are faced with circumstances they perceive to be risk-prone. According to researchers this is because the use of relations of trust in connection to commercial exchange, envelopes the exchange in a web of obligations and holds the seller's network hostage to appropriate role performance in relation to the transaction.

Trust and reciprocity appear to be quite closely linked. While trust can lead to relations of reciprocity, reciprocity can also lead to trust.

Transaction Costs

The concept of transaction costs is used to refer to costs incurred in the course of carrying out an economic exchange. Transaction cost theory is part of what has come to be known as new institutional economics. This line of economic theory expands neo-classical economic theories by incorporating property rights and transaction costs into neo-classical economics to explain economic behaviour.

Within the framework of standard transaction cost theory, transaction costs are often divided into different categories. Search or information costs refer to costs that are incurred while exploring whether the required good is to be found on the market, its costs, providers, and so forth. Bargaining or negotiation costs are the costs of negotiating and arriving at an agreement with the other party, as well as carrying out the transaction. Finally, the term enforce ment costs is used to refer to the costs of ensuring that the other party keeps his/her part of the agreement, and, if necessary, of taking action to this effect.

While new institutional economics places a stronger emphasis on empirical testing than, for example, standard neo-classical economics, it also has strong roots in rational choice theory. Some authors argue that this does not change the fact that transaction costs are difficult to measure in any objective way, and that the issue of what constitutes a transaction cost or not is specific to the circumstances and the parties involved.

In this chapter, the concept of transaction costs is used, in a broad sense, as an entry point for examining what, from a farmer's perspective, is regarded as a cost or a sacrifice incurred in relation to maize seed exchanges. It is argued that in farmer-to-farmer seed transactions the transaction costs are perceived by the farmers to be negligible.

4 Germination and Plant Growth

Germination is the process in which a plant or fungus emerges from a seed or spore and begins growth. The most common example of germination is the sprouting of a seedling from a seed of an angiosperm or gymnosperm. However, the growth of a sporeling from a spore, for example the growth of hyphae from fungal spores, is also germination. In a more general sense, germination can imply anything expanding into greater being from a small existence or germ.

Germination is the growth of an embryonic plant contained within a seed; it results in the formation of the seedling. The seed of a higher plant is a small package produced in a fruit or cone after the union of male and female sex cells. All fully developed seeds contain an embryo and, in most plant species some store of food reserves, wrapped in a seed coat. Some plants produce varying numbers of seeds that lack embryos, these are called empty seeds, and never germinate. Most seeds go through a period of quiescence where there is no active growth; during this time the seed can be safely transported to a new location and/or survive adverse climate conditions until circumstances are favourable for growth. Quiescent seeds are ripe seeds that do not germinate because they are subject to external environmental conditions that prevent the initiation of metabolic processes and cell growth. Under favourable conditions, the seed begins to germinate and the embryonic tissues resume growth, developing towards a seedling.

Factors Affecting Seed Germination

Seed germination depends on both internal and external conditions. The most important external factors include temperature, water, oxygen and sometimes light or darkness. Various plants require different variables for successful seed germination, often this depends on the individual seed variety and is closely linked to the ecological conditions of a plant's natural habitat. For some seeds, their future germination response is affected by environmental conditions during seed formation; most often these responses are types of seed dormancy.

- **Water** - is required for germination. Mature seeds are often extremely dry and need to take in significant amounts of water, relative to the dry weight of the seed, before cellular metabolism and growth can resume. Most seeds need enough water to moisten the seeds but not enough to soak them. The uptake of water by seeds is called imbibition, which leads to the swelling and the breaking of the seed coat. When seeds are formed, most plants store a food reserve with the seed, such as starch, proteins, or oils. This food reserve provides nourishment to the growing embryo. When the seed imbibes water, hydrolytic enzymes are activated which break down these stored food resources into metabolically useful chemicals. After the seedling emerges from the seed coat and starts growing roots and leaves, the seedling's food reserves are typically exhausted; at this point photosynthesis provides the energy needed for continued growth and the seedling now requires a continuous supply of water, nutrients, and light.
- **Oxygen** - is required by the germinating seed for metabolism. Oxygen is used in aerobic respiration, the main source of the seedling's energy until it grows leaves. Oxygen is an atmospheric gas that is found in soil pore spaces; if a seed is buried too deeply within the soil or the soil is waterlogged, the seed can be oxygen starved.

Some seeds have impermeable seed coats that prevent oxygen from entering the seed, causing a type of physical dormancy which is broken when the seed coat is worn away enough to allow gas exchange and water uptake from the environment.

- **Temperature** - affects cellular metabolic and growth rates. Seeds from different species and even seeds from the same plant germinate over a wide range of temperatures. Seeds often have a temperature range within which they will germinate, and they will not do so above or below this range. Many seeds germinate at temperatures slightly above room-temperature 60-75° F (16-24° C), while others germinate just above freezing and others germinate only in response to alternations in temperature between warm and cool. Some seeds germinate when the soil is cool 28-40° F (-2 - 4° C), and some when the soil is warm 76-90° F (24-32° C). Some seeds require exposure to cold temperatures (vernalization) to break dormancy. Seeds in a dormant state will not germinate even if conditions are favourable. Seeds that are dependent on temperature to end dormancy have a type of physiological dormancy. For example, seeds requiring the cold of winter are inhibited from germinating until they take in water in the fall and experience cooler temperatures. Four degrees Celsius is cool enough to end dormancy for most cool dormant seeds, but some groups, especially within the family Ranunculaceae and others, need conditions cooler than -5° C. Some seeds will only germinate after hot temperatures during a forest fire which cracks their seed coats; this is a type of physical dormancy.

Most common annual vegetables have optimal germination temperatures between 75-90° F (24-32° C), though many species (e.g. radishes or spinach) can germinate at significantly lower temperatures, as low as 40° F (4° C), thus allowing them to be grown from seed in cooler climates. Suboptimal temperatures lead to lower success rates and longer germination periods.

- **Light or darkness** - can be an environmental trigger for germination and is a type of physiological dormancy. Most seeds are not affected by light or darkness, but many seeds, including species found in forest settings, will not germinate until an opening in the canopy allows sufficient light for growth of the seedling.

Scarification mimics natural processes that weaken the seed coat before germination. In nature, some seeds require particular conditions to germinate, such as the heat of a fire (e.g., many Australian native plants), or soaking in a body of water for a long period of time. Others need to be passed through an animal's digestive tract to weaken the seed coat enough to allow the seedling to emerge.

Some live seeds are dormant and need more time, and/or need to be subjected to specific environmental conditions before they will germinate. Seed dormancy can originate in different parts of the seed, for example, within the embryo; in other cases the seed coat is involved. Dormancy breaking often involves changes in membranes, initiated by dormancy-breaking signals. This generally occurs only within hydrated seeds. Factors affecting seed dormancy include the presence of certain plant hormones, notably abscisic acid, which inhibits germination, and gibberellin, which ends seed dormancy. In brewing, barley seeds are treated with gibberellin to ensure uniform seed germination for the production of barley malt.

Seedling Establishment

In some definitions, the appearance of the radicle marks the end of germination and the beginning of "establishment", a period that ends when the seedling has exhausted the food reserves stored in the seed. Germination and establishment as an independent organism are critical phases in the life of a plant when they are the most vulnerable to injury, disease, and water stress. The germination index can be used as an indicator of phytotoxicity in soils. The mortality between dispersal of seeds and completion of establishment can be so high that many species have adapted to produce huge numbers of seeds.

Germination Rate

In agriculture and gardening, the germination rate describes how many seeds of a particular plant species, variety or seedlot are likely to germinate. It is usually expressed as a percentage, e.g., an 85 per cent germination rate indicates that about 85 out of 100 seeds will probably germinate under proper conditions. The germination rate is useful for calculating the seed requirements for a given area or desired number of plants.

Dicot Germination

The part of the plant that first emerges from the seed is the embryonic root, termed the radicle or primary root. It allows the seedling to become anchored in the ground and start absorbing water. After the root absorbs water, an embryonic shoot emerges from the seed. This shoot comprises three main parts: the cotyledons (seed leaves), the section of shoot below the cotyledons (hypocotyl), and the section of shoot above the cotyledons (epicotyl). The way the shoot emerges differs among plant groups.

Epigeous

In epigeous (or epigeal) germination, the *hypocotyl* elongates and forms a hook, pulling rather than pushing the cotyledons and apical meristem through the soil. Once it reaches the surface, it straightens and pulls the cotyledons and shoot tip of the growing seedlings into the air. Beans, tamarind, and papaya are examples of plants that germinate this way.

Hypogeous

Another way of germination is hypogeous (or hypogeal), where the epicotyl elongates and forms the hook. In this type of germination, the cotyledons stay underground where they eventually decompose. Peas, for example, germinate this way.

Monocot Germination

In monocot seeds, the embryo's radicle and cotyledon are covered by a coleorhiza and coleoptile, respectively. The coleorhiza is the first part to grow out of the seed, followed by the radicle. The coleoptile is then pushed up through the ground until it reaches the surface. There, it stops elongating and the first leaves emerge.

Precocious Germination

While not a class of germination, precocious germination refers to seed germination before the fruit has released seed. The seeds of the green apple commonly germinate in this manner.

Pollen Germination

Another germination event during the life cycle of gymnosperms and flowering plants is the germination of a pollen grain after pollination. Like seeds, pollen grains are severely dehydrated before being released to facilitate their dispersal from one plant to another. They consist of a protective coat containing several cells (up to 8 in gymnosperms, 2-3 in flowering plants). One of these cells is a tube cell. Once the pollen grain lands on the stigma of a receptive flower (or a female cone in gymnosperms), it takes up water and germinates. Pollen germination is facilitated by hydration on the stigma, as well as by the structure and physiology of the stigma and style. Pollen can also be induced to germinate *in vitro* (in a petri dish or test tube).

During germination, the tube cell elongates into a pollen tube. In the flower, the pollen tube then grows towards the ovule where it discharges the sperm produced in the pollen grain for fertilization. The germinated pollen grain with its two sperm cells is the mature male microgametophyte of these plants.

Self-incompatibility

Since most plants carry both male and female reproductive organs in their flowers, there is a high risk of self-pollination and thus inbreeding. Some plants use the control of pollen germination as a way to prevent this self-pollination. Germination and growth of the pollen tube involve molecular signaling between stigma and pollen. In self-incompatibility in plants, the stigma of certain plants can molecularly recognize pollen from the same plant and prevent it from germinating.

Spore Germination

Germination can also refer to the emergence of cells from resting spores and the growth of sporeling hyphae or thalli from spores in fungi, algae and some plants.

Conidia are asexual reproductive spores of fungi which germinate under specific conditions. A variety of cells can be formed from the germinating conidia. The most common are germ tubes which grow and develop into hyphae. Another type of cell is a conidial anastomosis tube (CAT); these differ from germ tubes in that they are thinner, shorter, lack branches, exhibit determinate growth and home toward each other. Each cell is of a tubular shape, but the conidial anastomosis tube forms a bridge that allows fusion between conidia.

Resting Spores

In resting spores, germination that involves cracking the thick cell wall of the dormant spore. For example, in zygomycetes the thick-walled zygosporangium cracks open and the zygospore inside gives rise to the emerging sporangiophore. In slime molds, germination refers to the emergence of amoeboid cells from the hardened spore. After cracking the spore coat, further development involves cell division, but not necessarily the development of a multicellular organism (for example in the free-living amoebas of slime molds).

Ferns and Mosses

In plants such as bryophytes, ferns, and a few others, spores germinate into independent gametophytes. In the bryophytes (e.g., mosses and liverworts), spores germinate into protonemata, similar to fungal hyphae, from which the gametophyte grows. In ferns, the gametophytes are small, heart-shaped prothalli that can often be found underneath a spore-shedding adult plant.

Seedling

A seedling is a young plant sporophyte developing out of a plant embryo from a seed. Seedling development starts with germination of the seed. A typical young seedling consists of three main parts: the radicle (embryonic root), the hypocotyl (embryonic shoot), and the cotyledons (seed leaves). The two classes of flowering plants are distinguished by their numbers of seed leaves: Monocotyledons (monocots) have one blade-shaped cotyledon, whereas dicotyledons (dicots) possess two round cotyledons. Gymnosperms are more varied. For example, pine seedlings have up to eight cotyledons. The seedlings of some flowering plants have no cotyledons at all. These are said to be acotyledons.

During germination, the young plant emerges from its protective seed coat with its radicle first, followed by the cotyledons. The radicle orients towards gravity, while the hypocotyl orients away from gravity and elongates through cell expansion to push the cotyledons out of the ground.

Photomorphogenesis and Etiolation

Dicot seedlings grown in the light develop short hypocotyls and open cotyledons exposing the epicotyl. This is also referred to as photomorphogenesis. In contrast, seedlings grown in the dark develop long hypocotyls and their cotyledons remain closed around the epicotyl in an *apical hook*. This is referred to as skotomorphogenesis or etiolation. Etiolated seedlings are yellowish in colour as chlorophyll synthesis and chloroplast development depend on light. They will open their cotyledons and turn green when treated with light.

In a natural situation, seedling development starts with skotomorphogenesis while the seedling is growing through the soil and attempting to reach the light as fast as possible. During this phase, the cotyledons are tightly closed and form the *apical hook* to protect the shoot apical meristem from damage while pushing through the soil. In many plants, the seed coat still covers the cotyledons for extra protection.

Upon breaking the surface and reaching the light, the seedling's developmental programme is switched to photomorphogenesis. The cotyledons open upon contact with light (splitting the seed coat open, if still present) and become green, forming the first photosynthetic organs of the young plant. Until this stage, the seedling lives off the energy reserves stored in the seed. The opening of the cotyledons exposes the shoot apical meristem and the *plumule* consisting of the first *true leaves* of the young plant.

The seedlings sense light through the light receptors phytochrome (red and far-red light) and cryptochrome (blue light). Mutations in these photo receptors and their signal transduction components lead to seedling development that is at odds with light conditions, for example seedlings that show photomorphogenesis when grown in the dark.

Seedling Growth and Maturation

Once the seedling starts to photosynthesize, it is no longer dependent on the seed's energy reserves. The apical meristems start growing and give rise to the root and shoot. The first "true" leaves expand and can often be distinguished from the round cotyledons through their species-dependent distinct shapes. While the plant is growing and developing additional leaves, the cotyledons eventually senesce and fall off. Seedling growth is also affected by mechanical stimulation, such as by wind or other forms of physical contact, through a process called thigmomorphogenesis.

5 Maize Cultivation

Maize is one of the three cereals, together with rice and wheat, that make up the backbone of the world's food supply. The versatile use of maize furthermore, means that over the next decades the importance of maize will increase even further. Considering the less than impressive cob of the ancestor of maize, teosinte, this was far from a foregone conclusion and exactly how it happened is still being debated. Part of the explanation is found in the biology of maize, and in particular in how it reproduces, and how it interacts with the environment. All of these issues directly or indirectly play a part in the maize seed systems of small-scale farmers in Oaxaca, and the following chapter provides a short overview primarily targeted at readers new to maize.

Maize is one of the world's most important crops. Measured in terms of area harvested or in terms of its global average contribution to human daily calorie intake, maize ranks third after wheat and rice; however, measured in terms of total production, it is the most important cereal crop.

Maize is grown around the world from 50 degrees north to 50 degrees south; from sea level to altitudes above 3,000 masl, on flat lands and steep slopes, and in climates ranging from tropical to temperate and from semi-arid to extremely wet. In this sense, maize is today the world's most widely grown cereal, a fact that reflects its ability to adapt to a wide range of agricultural environments.

Approximately 69 per cent or 99 of the 144 million hectares of maize in the world are grown in the developing world according to FAO. Nevertheless, only about 44 per cent of the global maize harvest is produced in this part of the world. A wide gap in average maize yields/ha continues to exist between the developed world and the developing world Global maize demand is projected to increase by 50 per cent from 1995 to 2020. By 2020 maize demand in the developing world is expected to exceed the demand for both wheat and rice. In the developing world alone the demand is expected to increase almost 80 per cent. Rising incomes in certain parts of the developing world, and with that, increased consumption of meat and poultry, particularly in East and Southeast Asia, is resulting in growing demand for maize as animal feed.

In other parts of the developing world maize continues to be the most important food crop and the source for more than a quarter of the average daily calorie intake per capita, for example, in Eastern and southern Africa as well as in Central America and the Caribbean. In Sub-Saharan Africa, Central America and parts of South Asia, the persistence of poverty in combination with continued population growth is expected to continue upward pressure on maize demand for human consumption. In Sub-Saharan Africa, for example, the annual maize demand is expected to double between 1995 and 2020, and in many Latin American countries the demand for food maize continues to be high.

No other crop produces so much food per unit of land or labour as maize and no other cereal crop has so many uses as maize. Maize also plays an important role in relation to global food security. This is particularly the case in Africa and Latin America, where maize makes up a significant part of the overall daily per capita calorie intake. In Zambia, Lesotho and Malawi, maize contributes more than 50 per cent of the average daily calorie intake, while in the Americas, in countries like Guatemala, Mexico, El Salvador and Honduras, maize remains the source of more than 30 per cent of the average calorie intake per capita per day.

Meanwhile, the demand for maize as livestock feed, mainly for poultry and pigs, is growing significantly, as the living standards in several developing countries, especially in Asia, is rising and the demand for meat and eggs increase.

In addition to its importance as a food crop and its value as animal feed, maize has several other diverse uses both in a rural household and in industry, Whether fresh or processed, maize can be used as food for humans, as feed for animals, as a raw material in the industrial production of starch, oil, sugar, protein, cellulose, ethylic alcohol, as construction material, for fuel, mulching, for the artisanal fabrication of handicrafts and tools.

In the industrialized world, the role of maize as human food is minimal. The major role of maize in this part of the world is as feed, mainly for cattle, pigs and poultry, and as raw material in a number of extractive industries. As researcher points out, maize is therefore a significant if indirect input in the production of meat, eggs, milk, cheese and butter, as well as in an endless list of other products. Among others researcher lists products as diverse as whiskey, chewing gum and soft drinks, toothpaste, shaving cream, shoe polish, detergents, rayon, rubber tires, explosives and embalming fluid.

The Origin and Spread of Maize

The Origin of Maize

Maize is unknown in the wild and maize as we know it today is unable to survive without human interference. The maize cob is so tightly wrapped in the husks and the seeds so tightly compacted and attached to the cob that maize is unable to reproduce itself without the farmer's help. Even if a whole ear is buried and left to sprout, the young shoots will overcrowd each other and perish. As Wallace and Brown comment for maize to survive on its own more than two years without human intervention would be astounding. The origin of maize has been much debated in the past, and several theories regarding its ancestry and place of origin and domestication have been proposed These often feature other members of the *Maydeae* tribe such as teosinte, the common name for a group of annual and perennial species of the genus *Zea*, and tripsacum, *Zea*'s sister genus. Among the early theories, one argued that maize was developed from teosinte with the help of early humans. Other hypotheses held that cultivated maize was domesticated from an earlier, hypothetical 'wild maize', which had later become extinct, and that teosinte on the other hand was the result of hybridization of maize and tripsacum or, as was later suggested, from the hybridization of maize and perennial teosinte.

In addition, the extraordinary morphological and genetic diversity of maize, as well as its widespread cultivation in the Americas at the time of the conquest, lead some scientists to suggest that maize domestication had taken place independently in multiple locations.

Today, however, teosinte is widely recognized by scientists as the ancestor of maize.

Furthermore, studies using multilocus microsatelite genotyping, a technique that was unavailable until a few years ago, have produced strong indications that maize evolved from a single domestication, and that this took place approximately 9,000 years ago in Southern Mexico. Moreover, the research by Matsuoka et al. clearly indicated the progenitor of maize to be *Zea parviglumis,* which is a subspecies of teosinte The evolution of maize from teosinte is highly unlikely to have taken place without human interference, and it is widely believed today, that humans were a crucial selective agent in the evolution and domestication of maize. As a result of, on the one hand favourable natural mutations and hybridization between different types of maize, and on the other hand farmers' selection for ear and grain size, as well as colour, and other kernel and plant characteristics, maize evolved from a wild plant with a small, self-sowing type of 'ear', into a highly productive plant with multi-rowed ears enclosed in a protective husk and with multiple uses.

The oldest known remains of domesticated maize were found in the Guila Naquitz cave in the Central Valleys of Oaxaca and date back approximately 6250 years, according to researchers. Before researchers reanalysis of the finds from Guila Naquitz, the earliest maize cobs known were thought to be from Tehuacan on the border between researchers. No crops are thought to have been domesticated in Mexico earlier than 10,000 years ago. Hence, it is estimated that maize was domesticated between 6000 and 10,000 years ago. This is consistent with indications from molecular dating analysis, which suggests that maize was domesticated in Southern Mexico about 9000 years ago.

The fact that the oldest archaeological maize finds are from Oaxaca, points in the direction of Oaxaca as the area of domestication of maize. However, it is not unlikely that even older maize remains may be found elsewhere in the future.

Zea parviglumis is a contemporary teosinte subspecies. It is still found in the wild between 400 and 1800 masl in the Rio Balsas region, along the western escarpment of Mexico from Nayarit to Oaxaca.Within the highlands of Southern Mexico, Oaxaca and the area of the Rio Balsas watershed on the border between the states of Michoacan and Guererro are both regarded as possible locations for maize domestication.

However, of the teosintes found today, the type most closely related to maize is found in the Rio Balsas region. This may be seen as pointing in the direction of this area as the location of maize domestication, although it should be noted that the modern distribution of teosinte populations may not be the same as during the domestication period.

Mexico is widely recognized as a centre of diversity for maize. Though ancient maize remains have been found elsewhere in the Americas, none of these are thought to predate the earliest Mexican finds. The presence of *Zea parviglumis* in modern day Mexico, and the results of various studies using modern population genetic analysis and other advanced technologies, furthermore point convincingly to Southern Mexico as the original cradle of maize.

Numerous artefacts and other archaeological evidence testify to the importance of maize in the ancient cultures of the Americas.

At the time of the Europeans' arrival, maize was grown in large parts of the American continent. The analyses of researcher indicate two main routes of maize's dispersal throughout the Americas. One took maize through western and northern Mexico into the south-west of the US, from where it continued to spread eastwards and north into Canada and the eastern US. Meanwhile a south-bound route went through the western and southern Statue with maize ear headdress and a maize ear in each hand. The figure's protruding lips, elliptical eye shape and ear rings are characteristic of Oaxacan funerary urns. Based on the characteristics of the maize, the piece is suspected of being post-Columbian.

Urn depicting the God Cocijo with a collar of maize ears; period Monte Alban IV (A.D. 750-1000), Museo Nacional de Antropologia 6-6758, here from Eubanks, 1999. God of Lightening and Rain, Cocijo was the most important deity in the Zapotec pantheon. "Since maize was the mainstay of pre-Columbian life and the development and survival of urban society depended on its successful production, this divinity, who controlled the elements on which the success of maize and other crops depended, was ofparamount importance".

Lowlands of Mexico into Central America and the Caribbean Islands and from there into the lowlands of South America and finally the Andean region. In addition, archaeological evidence suggests continued contact and exchanges through time between populations of Meso- and

South America, which may well have included maize. Maize continued to develop alongside pre-columbian civilizations and became one of the most important food staples, if not *the* most important, in much of pre-hispanic America. Indeed, as researcher comments, it has been suggested that hybridization of maize from Meso- and South America, resulting in more productive and higher yielding races better equipped for adaptation to different agro-ecological conditions may have played an important role in terms of increased food supply, which in turn may have accelerated population growth and the development of these civilizations.

On the 5 of November, 1492, two members of Columbus' crew returned from an expedition into the interior of Cuba. Among other things they reported that the natives had a kind of grain, they called 'mahiz', which tasted good and which they baked, dried and made into flour. The two crew members were probably the first Europeans to have seen the plant which has since become one of the world's most important food crops, not to mention its importance in numerous other respects - as researchers comment, "a cereal treasure of immensely greater value than the spices, which Columbus travelled so far to seek". When he returned from his first journey in 1493, Columbus brought kernels of yellow flint maize from Cuba to Spain where it was received with much interest. According to researchers, what arrived with Columbus as a botanical curiosity, became an important commercial field crop within just a hundred years, and was widely grown in Spain, Italy and southern France by the end of the 1500s.

Its high multiplication ratio and high yield potential spurred maize's spread from Europe to Asia and Africa with the explorers and traders of the 16 century. By the mid 1700s maize had established a strong foothold in west and central Africa where it had even started to displace other food crops; it had also spread to south and south-east Asia and was a well-established crop in several of the southern Chinese provinces.

Meanwhile in North America, need led European settlers to adopt this 'Indian corn' which they regarded with a certain disdain, as a substitute for wheat. As Wallace and Brown put it, maize became "the bridge by which the pioneers crossed America to the Missouri", and "decade after decade, beginning in 1780, the progress of American civilization was measured by the western expansion of the corn acreage".

Maize Breeding Basics

Throughout in this section, researchers refers to different types of maize populations, including landraces, creolized varieties and modern or 'improved' varieties. The term maize population can be used as a generic term for any group of maize plants under management by breeders or farmers. 'Landrace' is used to refer to "a locally grown maize population that has been the result of farmer selection and management over many generations".

An 'improved or modern variety' is a maize population that has been scientifically bred and conforms to the International Union for the Protection of New Varieties of Plants, UPOV, criteria of being distinct, uniform and stable. A creolized variety is an originally improved variety that has been under farmer management for several generations.

The term 'farmer variety' is sometimes used to refer to a crop population that a group of farmers recognize as a distinct unit, regardless of whether it is a landrace, an 'improved' or creolized variety. They may, or may not, have specific names beyond the colour of the kernel. 'Farmer variety' contrasts with the variety concept used in the context of developed country agriculture, where a 'variety' is defined as a plant grouping within a single botanical taxon of the lowest rank; this grouping can be defined by the expression of characteristics resulting from a given genotype or combination of genotypes.

Open Pollinated Variety (OPV)

In self-pollinating crops, for example wheat and rice, pollination of the ovules of each individual plant happens with pollen from the same plant. The genetic make-up of the crop population remains largely unchanged from one generation to the next. However, maize is an open-pollinated crop. This means that the ovules of each plant are largely pollinated by pollen from other maize plants, or, put in a different way, that the male and female heritage is contributed by two different plants. Under natural circumstances maize reproduction therefore entails a high degree of exchange of genetic material between plants.

When the silks of a maize plant are fertilized by pollen from the same plant, scientists refer to the resulting kernels as *inbred*. Inbreeding decreases genetic variability, thereby increasing the uniformity of the maize in this case. However, inbreeding also increases the frequency of deleterious mutations, which can lead to a decline in plant vigour in species,like maize, that are normally open-pollinated. According to researchers, after three generations of systematic, targeted inbreeding, maize will yield only half as much as usual, though it will be very uniform. A similar effect sometimes occurs in farmers' fields, though normally over a much longer time span.

If the farmer, who selects and saves seed from his/her own maize harvest year after year, selects all the seed from a very limited number of cobs, the genetic variation of the seed lot may eventually become so limited that the frequency of deleterious mutations will increase and inbreeding depression will be the result. Mexican small-scale farmers will sometimes refer to this phenomenon by saying that the maize has become tired (*cansado*).

While maize self-pollination or inbreeding tends to produce offspring that underperform their parents, the crossing of genetically different maize plants tends to produce offspring that perform better than their parents. This phenomenon is known as *hybrid vigour* or heterosis. In their own way farmers sometimes make use of this phenomenon. When Mexican smallscale farmers consider that their maize has become 'tired', they will sometimes deliberately mix their maize with another kind of maize in order to make their own maize 'stronger' (*para reforzar el maíz*).

In principle the term hybrid simply refers to an animal or a plant produced from genetically distinct parents. However, maize scientists have combined the mechanisms of both inbreeding and hybrid vigour in the creation of what has come to be known as *hybrid maize*. The use of inbreeding serves to limit the genetic variability and enhance the homogeneity of lines used as parents;and the c rossing of genetically distinct parents are used to achieve hybrid vigour. Many different types of hybrid maize exists; as an example, a singlecross hybrid is produced by crossing two distinct inbred parents: Inbred A × inbred B = single-cross hybrid AB.

The first generation of a hybrid will exhibit more vigourous growth, yield or disease resistance than either of its parents. However, the hybrid vigour effect tends to decline in subsequent generations. Though the degree of this decline varies between the different types of hybrids, single-cross hybrids are oftcn highly unstable and may exhibit yield declines of 25-40 per cent or more already in the second generation. This may not prove a problem in areas where a well-developed formal seed sector exists, and farmers are able to buy fresh commercial seed every year. However, yield stability is an important issue in relation to hybrid maize seed in areas where farmers do not have reliable access to seed supply or are accustomed to selecting and recycling seed from their previous harvest.

Another popular strategy for the development of improved maize varieties consists of routinely crossing genetically diverse maize types in order to develop maize populations, which are then improved through recurrent selection.

This category of improved maize is normally referred to as OPVs or *open-pollinated varieties*. According to the CIMMYT Maize Programme an OPV can be defined as an assemblage of phenotypes that is different, relatively uniform and stable. As mentioned above, all maize is naturally open pollinated. However, the use of the term OPV refers to the fact that seed is produced by open (uncontrolled) pollination, as opposed to hybrid varietieswhich require controlled pollination.

Modern hybrid maize demonstrates a yield advantage in comparison to improved OPVs. However, while studies have shown best hybrids to be superior over best OPVs by an average of 15-20 per cent, improved OPVs do not show the dramatic declines in yield characteristic of hybrids, in subsequent generations. For example, Pixley and Banzinger, (2004) found the effect of planting recycled seed to be negligible for OPVs, severe for hybrids (>30%) and intermediate for topcross hybrids (approximately 16%).

OPVs have an important role in maize agriculture in developing countries. Compared to hybrid maize, improved OPVs are easier to develop and their seed production is simpler and relatively inexpensive. Furthermore, farmers can recycle the seed of OPVs for 3-4 years with only negligible to minimal yield declines. Thus, instead of buying new seed every year, it is only necessary to buy new seed every 3-4 years, a fact that significantly reduces farmers' dependence on external seed sources. Furthermore, as management and input requirements for OPVs are similar to those of many local landraces used by poor maize farmers, farmer-to-farmer seed flow is relatively uncomplicated.

Genotype-by-environment Interaction

Environmental factors play an important role in crop performance; however, some crops respond more strongly than others across different environments.

Maize exhibits what plant breeders call a high *genotype-by-environment interaction* or GxE, meaning that its' performance across different agro-ecological environments depends on its specific genetic make-up. In other words, a genotype, that is, the specific genetic constitution of a certain maize 'variety', which performs well in one environment, may not do so in another. The ability to perform under extremely diverse growing conditions reflects the impressive morphological and genetic diversity in maize, which enables this crop to adapt to a wide range of environments. At the same time, though, maize's genotype-environment sensitivity also means that, often, a maize 'variety' that is well adapted to a specific growing environment will not perform satisfactorily if introduced into a markedly different agro-ecological context.

A process of adaptation is sometimes possible which can mitigate this, for example, through farmers' selection or what breeders call adaptive breeding. However, the essence of maize's high genotype-by-environment interaction is that different maize 'varieties' are appropriate and will perform well in different agro-ecological environments. For formal maize breeding purposes this also means that maize breeding efforts must be targeted carefully to relatively specific agro-ecological conditions. For example, the hybrid maize varieties that are popular in the American Midwest are not appropriate in the tropics – in fact, they may not even be able to produce viable seed. This has important implications for farmers, who must make sure that the varieties they plant are appropriate for the particular agro-ecological conditions present on the farm.

Maize's scientific name is *Zea mays* L. Like all the major cereals, it is a grass. In botanical terms, maize forms part of the *Gramineae* family, within which it belongs to the *Maydeae* tribe.

A mature maize plant normally has a single dominant stalk. The stalk has between 8 and 20 nodes from each of which a leaf emerges on alternate sides of the stalk. The part between the nodes is called the internode and is where growth takes place. The roots of maize are thestrongest of all annual crop plants. The main roots may penetrate as much as 1.5-1.8 metre into the ground and 0.9-1.2 metre sideways. In addition maize often features brace roots beginning 2-3 nodes above the ground.

While some types of maize barely reach a maximum height of one metre, others grow to more than 5 times this height. At the top the stalk ends in a tassel with 5-20 branches, each with hundreds of little spikelets, which are the male flowers of the maize plant. From nodes along the stem several ear shoots may develop, each covered by a protective layer of husk leaves. While most of the ear shoots degenerate, one or two will continue to develop into the female inflorescence of the maize plant. The maize plants' ability to convert sunlight, water, air and soil into biomass is extraordinary. In about 3 months a single maize seed can develop into a plant more than 5 metres tall, carrying more than 1000 seeds.

When flowering time approaches, a tuft of silks will protrude from the tip of the ear. Each silk is connected to an ovule on the maize cob, and each ovule is a potential maize kernel. Ovules and silks make up the female element of the maize plant. Each spikelet on the tassel contains a number of pollen sacs, also called anthers.

When these ripen they begin to shed pollen - the male element of the maize plant. The moment a pollen grain lands on a silk, it starts to travel down through the silk for 20-25 cm to the ovule, where the pollinization is completed.can vary considerably, and depends, in part, on the number of rows of kernels on the cob. Some cobs have only 8 rows, while others can have up to 30 rows. Similarly, maize ears come in different sizes ranging from 7.5-40 cm long.

The shape of maize kernels depends on the type of maize in question. Dented maize has wrinkled or indented kernels; flintmaize has smooth kernels; and floury maize has smooth-slightly dented kernels.

Maize kernels can be different colours; including white, yellow, black and red, and for each of these different nuances may apply. Finally, some maize is of mixed colour, that is, produce ears with kernels of 2-4 different colours, for example, white-and-black, or white-black-and-yellow.

Only in yellow maize does the pigment that gives the kernel its particular colour reside in the endosperm; in black/blue, red and white maize the pigmentation is limited to a thin layer just below the pericarp and covering the endosperm. The oblong centre of the maize kernel is the germ, that is, the dormant seedling from which a new maize plant will grow. It is surrounded by the endosperm, a body of starch which serves as nutrition for the germinating seedling. The kernel is covered by a thin membrane called the pericarp, and is attached to the cob by the pedicel. On average a maize kernel contains 72 per cent starch, 10 per cent protein, 3 per cent sugar, 4.8 per cent oil, 8.5 per cent fibre and 1.7 per cent ash, of which the oil is contained in the germ, while the rest are in the surrounding endosperm.

6 Seed Production and Management

Introduction

In hybrid seed production, the crosses are specific and controlled. The advantage of growing hybrid seed compared to inbred lines comes from heterosis. To produce hybrid seed, elite inbred varieties are crossed with well-documented and consistent phenotypes (such as yield) and the resulting hybrid seed is collected.

Another factor that is important in hybrid seed production is the combining ability of the parent plants. Although two elite inbred parent plant varieties may produce the highest yields of their crop, it does not necessarily mean that crossing these inbreds will result in the highest yielding hybrid. The level of heterosis that the parents will generate in the resultant seed is called "combining ability." Higher combining ability between the parents results in increased performance in the resulting hybrid seed.

Hybrids are bred to improve the characteristics of the resulting plants, such as better yield, greater uniformity, improved colour, disease resistance, and so forth. Today, hybrid seed production is predominant in agriculture and home gardening, and is one of the main contributing factors to the dramatic rise in agricultural output during the last half of the 20th century. In the US, the commercial market was launched in the 1920s, with the first hybrid maize. All of the hybrid seeds planted by the farmer will be the same hybrid while the seeds from the hybrids planted will not consistently have the desired characteristics. This is why hybrid seed is constantly repurchased by growers for each planting season.

- The first coordinated crop improvement project was launched on maize by ICAR in 1957. Large number of inbred lines and hybrids were introduced from USA and corn belt region.
- These inbred lines along side with exotic and indigenous hybrids were tried in multilocational trials.
- As a result 28 inbreds were picked up for utilization in hybrid development.
- Some exotic hybrids particularly from Southern USA (NC 27, Texas 26 and Dixie 18) displayed significantly higher yield but were not accepted by the Indian farmers due to their dent type grain.
- These dent type hybrids also had a problem in seed production, as their parental lines were adapted to temperate climate.
- Realising these difficulties, Indian germplasm collection was intensified.
- The local land races collected were yellow flint grain type, obviously preferred by Indian farmers.
- After characterisation and classification of Indian land races and simultaneous effects for extracting inbred lines both from indigenous and exotic materials, first set of yellow double cross hybrids were released in 1961.
- Though these hybrids performed very well in the farmers fields, success was limited by the problem encountered in their economic seed production.
- To tie this problem a short-term approach odd developing non-conventional hybrids (Double top cross hybrids and hybrids involving early generation inbreds) was immediately adopted.
- As a result in 1963 two double top cross hybrids (Histarch, ganga-safed-2) were released.

- Also, composites and synthetic population were synthesized with the objectives of raising the levels of base population for developing agronomically better inbreds and for the commercial cultivation.
- Presently over 20 hybrids (Including double cross, double top cross and three way cross) besides many composites and synthetics are released to the farmer for their commercial exploitation.
- Kisan, Jawahar, Sona, Vijaya, Amber and vikram were released in 1967. Vijay become popular not only in India but also in neighboring countries like Pakistan and Nepal.
- To enhance the performance of composite varieties by accumulating favourable alle Intra-population improvement programme at the national level was initiated in ten elite composites of various maturity groups.
- Five broad based gene pools in two grain colours yellow and white (AB yellow, AB white , BC yellow, CD yellow, CD white) were constituted to develop promising varieties and hybrids.

Hybrid Seed Production

- Breeders have developed high yielding varieties or hybrids of maize. Those improved stains have made a major contribution to increased food grain production.
- Maize hybrids are more attractive to seed industry for the economic reasons namely, higher profit margin for seed producers and farmer must return to buy new hybrid seed each year.
- Use of hybrid maize has resulted in the development of a new enterprise the production, processing sale and distribution of Hybrid seed.
- Thus the seed production today is a specialized and essential industry. It is analogous to fertilizer or pesticide industry.

- The seed industry is made up of several components including research production, quality control and marketing.
- Production of high quality seed is the primary objective of a seed programme.
- Care is to be taken to fix certification standards for various stages of seed multiplication to produce quality seed with out hampering seed production.
- When an improved strain is developed and performs well enough for use by the cultivators, it is proposed for release.
- The plant breeder provides its specific genetical and morphological characters based on which the cultivar is identified.

Maize Hybrid seed production consists of three stages. They are:

- Breeder seed.
- Foundation seed.
- Certified seed.

Breeder Seed

- Production of breeder seed is directly controlled by the plant Breeder.
- This stage of seed production is called "Breeders seed".
- It is generally produced in limited area either by hand pollination or in isolation.

Foundation Seed

- Foundation seed generally consists of production of single crosses by sowing male and female parents.
- These parents will be sown in 2:4 row ratio.
- Destasselling will be done in female rows.
- All off types, diseased and rogues if any found will be removed.

- Certification standards will be maintained under the guidance of monitoring team consisting of National seed corporation agencies, Certification, Agencies, Breeders and I.C.A.R. Nominee.

Certified Seed

- Certified seed i.e. the last stage of Maize hybrid seed production.
- Male and female single crosses are generally sown on 2:6 ratio.
- Female plants are detasseled.
- All off types, diseased and rogues if any found will be removed.
- Certification standards will be maintained under the guidance of monitoring team. The seed obtained on female rows is called certified seed.
- This seed is labeled as hybrid seed and sold to the farmers for commercial cultivation

Factors Affecting Maize Seed Production

Planting ratio

- At present uniform planting ratio of 2:4 for foundation seed production and 2:6 for certified seed production plots has been recommended.
- Maize inbreds vary considerably in respect of plant height, Panicle size, the amount of pollen produced and duration of pollen availability.
- Some time this factor may pose some problem to the producers.

Non-synchronization of flowering

- Good seed set in seed parent can be achieved by chronological adjustment of pollen shedding and silking respectively.
- Prolongation of effective flowering period, planting design, efficient alteration of rows planting ratio,

staggered planting are some of measures which are effectively used to ensure maximum synchronisation and good seed set.

Genetic Drift

- It is recognised as a important factor affecting quality of seed.
- The danger of genetic change in respect of cross pollinated crops like maize is prominent.
- Plants of different types permitted in a line may be susceptible to selection resulting in complete shift in the average perform and of a line over a period of time if produced repeatedly in smaller plots.

Detasseling

- All tassles must be removed from the female rows before they have shed any pollen. Pulling the tassels usually as soon as they are well out of the boot is the most satisfactory method of removal.

Mutation

- Aging of seed under storage is reported to have increased frequencies of chromosomal aberrations and point mutation.

Mechanical Admixtures

- These can be avoided taking due precaution at harvesting, seed setting, bagging and storing operations etc.

Rouging

· Based on distinct and diagnostic characters furnished by the breeder, rouging has to be performed in seedling stage flowering stage and at the time of harvesting (Plant and Ear Characters).

Physiological Maturity of the Crop

- The crop should be harvested at proper stage of maturity to minimise qualitative & quantitative losses.

Seed Size

- Grading of seed is important as it avoids smaller seed, under developed and damaged seeds.
- Smaller seeds had good germination but under stress condition the performance was significantly effected.

Storage

- Proper care for aeration temperature and humidity etc. should be taken from time to time.

Limit for Breeder Seed Indent

- Large indents of breeder seeds are not being entertained from the seed producing agencies.
- As there is a provision for stage I and stage II line increase, no producer should be permitted to indent more than 4 to 5 kg per inbred in a year.
- If the total indent for a inbred comes to 30 to 40 kg per year, it will be possible for the breeder to multiply a quintal or two of each inbred and store them so that he does not have to multiply them in large quantities every year.
- This will also ensure against the possibility of gene shift due to the frequent multiplication of any inbred.

Limitations of Hybrids

- Varieties with superior performance can be produced at each cycle of development as opposed to the substantial time log required for hybrid development.
- Since base populations and varieties improve proportionally with each selection cycle, after a given number of cycles there is very little difference in the expected performance of hybrids varieties.
- In fact it pays if adequate selected is practiced in each cycle, varieties can be superior to hybrid performance after any fixed period of time.
- To obtain anticipated potential yield of hybrids, new seed must be obtained each season from a specific source.

- However, the lack of an appropriate infrastructure for seed production and distribution in many developing nations make the use of hybrids a more difficult proposition.
- In contrast the relatively easy reproducibility of varieties makes such material more appropriate in these nations.
- In the event of poor quality or untimely seed distribution by the not so well organized seed corporation, the farmers themselves can save their variety seed for the next planting and even subsequent seasons if necessary.
- Farmer to farmer distributions of seed is possible if varieties sown by them are with desirable isolation distances. Seed increase is also more rapid than with hybrids.
- Costs lower in seed production of varieties since it requires only on isolation while in case of hybrids they need 5 to 7 isolations and cost of production is more.
- Varieties can be served as base material to develop parental lines and also can be used as a male parent in making double top cross hybrid.
- Varieties are more stable than hybrids in areas of varying rainfall and high soil variability.
- They are recommended for adverse conditions. Since they have broad genetic base in their makeup.
- Desirable attributes say resistance to a disease can be introgressed in the varieties very conveniently.

In the last two decades, researchers have come up with many new production technologies for different cropping systems. The growing of improved varieties, mineral fertilizer use, rotations, and intercrops, have all boosted production considerably. Nevertheless, the gains of technological advancement are threatened by poor post-production techniques to process, handle and store the increased production. Due to high levels of investment in crop production, post-harvest losses, in the form of quantity or quality, should be kept at a minimum.

Quantity losses can occur because of inconsistent harvest methods, spillage during transportation, or damage by pest organisms causing reductions in weight or volume. Quality losses can occur as changes in colour, smell or taste; contamination with toxins, pathogens, insects or rodent excreta; reduction in nutritional value; or loss of viability if the harvest is meant for seed.

Your Major Enemies to Stored Grain

1. **Insect pests:** Despite timely harvest, proper drying and shelling, and hygienic conditions, various pests still infest harvested grain. Insects are generally the most serious pests of stored grain. Storage insects are generally small in body size, rarely exceeding 2 mm in length, making them difficult to detect unless they are numerous. However, they have the capacity to multiply rapidly, so that in a very short space of time, you can easily have thousands of them attacking your grain. This rapid population growth makes them the major cause of food loss in stored grain. They are well adapted to darkness, and to movement in confined spaces and amongst stored grain. Many insect species can be found in association with stored grain, but only some are of economic importance. The most frequently encountered insect pests on stored maize include:
    - The Grain weevil (Sitophilus zeamais), which can fly and the Granary weevil (Sitophilus granarius), which cannot fly.
    - Angoumois Grain Moths (Sitotroga cerealella).
    - Grain borers: Larger grain borer (Prostephanus truncates) and the lesser grain borer (Rhyzopertha dominica).
    - Termites, which cause serious damage to the maize crop at all stages, from seedlings through to stored grain.
2. **Microorganisms:** Virtually all environments are surrounded by large populations of microorganisms,

including bacteria, fungi and yeasts. Some enter the grain, while others contaminate or damage it from outside. Microorganisms can attack stored grain before it dries properly, when the storage environment is moist, or when it accumulates moisture. Typically, grain attacked by bacteria develops a foul rotting smell, while yeasts cause a musty, fermented smell and a slimy texture. Fungal infection is the most widespread in stored grain and appears as mold or caking on the affected ear or grain. The grain loses colour, and there is loss of viability and reduction in food value. The most feared by-product of fungal attack is the production of poisonous substances called mycotoxins. Mycotoxins cause poisoning in both livestock and people.

3. **Domestic rodents:** This group, mainly rats and mice, causes some of the heaviest losses to stored grain. They feed on stored produce and prefer foods rich in proteins and oil, such that they may simply eat the germ of maize grain and leave the rest of the seed. A rat can eat an amount of food equivalent to about 7per cent of its body weight daily, (i.e. leading to losses of approximately 7 kg of grain per year). They also contaminate produce with urine, feces and other pathogens such as fleas. It is usually impossible to remove these contaminants and infested grain becomes spoiled and unfit for human consumption.

What to do to Reduce Post-harvest Losses

The first step in managing post-harvest losses begins at planting. Some maize varieties are more susceptible to attack than others. Research has produced many improved hybrid varieties tolerant to a number of pests and diseases. In addition, some traditional varieties are resistant to some pests such as the maize weevil, and it may be important to identify those varieties. At harvest, it is important to be aware of possible sources of pest infestation. Likely sources of infestation include infestation from field to storage, insects/

microorganisms remaining from previously stored grain, and cross contamination to a cleanly harvested lot. Upon identification in the field, an infested crop should can be cleaned or destroyed before harvest. The storage structure should also be cleaned thoroughly before depositing your harvest. The storage structure should be dusted with a pesticide, especially if a previous infestation was experienced. Be on the lookout for any possible hiding places for insects, while traps or baits can be set up for rodents.

7
Planning Seed Collection

Introduction

Species which bear ripe seed in adequate quantities at all times present little problem to the experienced seed collector, but such species are few. Some species bear seed throughout the year but only a little at any one time e.g. *P. merkusii* in Indonesia and this makes seed collection slow and expensive. In the majority of species the seeding season is concentrated within a few weeks and the collector's objective is to collect as much of the crop as possible within the short period while the seeds are mature but the fruits have not yet fallen or dehisced. Large indehiscent or fleshy fruits may be collected from the ground but even in these cases collection must be done quickly to avoid losses from animals, fungi or premature germination. Prior planning of collecting activities is therefore essential in order to ensure that operations are conducted as quickly and efficiently as possible in the limited time available. Collection in accessible and easily observable plantations or seed orchards reduces the need for careful preparation. On the other hand, collection in inaccessible, multispecific natural forests or sampling a number of different seed sources within a widely spread species calls for very careful planning if trained collecting teams are to operate with the right equipment in the right place at the right time. International seed expeditions encounter special problems, as they often operate in several different countries, each with its own regulations, and they seek to supply the varying needs of many using countries.

Determining Species, Provenances and Stands

Species

Selection of species for planting often presents no problem. In a simple afforestation project, which uses a proven well adapted species and provenance and obtains the seed from a local seed source, the choice is automatic. But not infrequently afforestation objectives change, e.g. emphasis may shift from sawlog to pulpwood or fuelwood production, or unexpected disease problems may arise. In East Africa *Pinus radiata* featured prominently in planting programmes until it was severely attacked by the needle blight *Dothistroma pini* in the 1960's. Thereafter its large-scale planting had to be abandoned and the planting programmes of resistant species, such as *P. patula* and *Cupressus lusitanica*, were expanded in compensation.

For large-scale collections, data on seed demands by species need to be assembled some months in advance. Most species need a year or more in the nursery. Estimates of seed demand must therefore be made about two years before planting in the field. Only rarely will the seed collectors and the seed users be the same persons. More often, whether collection is done by forest services or by private collectors, they will be supplying the needs of several different users. A centralised organisation is needed to solicit demand estimates from the several planting agencies and to consolidate these by species and provenance. Consolidated regional or global estimates of seed demand are much more difficult to compile than those for single countries, but recently attempts have been made to do this for tropical conifers and for western North American conifers.

Provenances

The word "provenance" has been used in somewhat different ways by different authors. In its simplest use, it is "The place in which any stand of trees is growing". When applied to seeds, the meaning is frequently extended to include "The area where the mother trees of the seeds were growing". In cases where seeds are collected from an exotic plantation or "derived provenance", there has been some inconsistency in usage; some authors would define provenance as the place in which the immediate parents were growing as exotics, others would confine its use to the place where the original progenitors were growing in natural forest. Provided that seed origin data give the data on the full pedigree, including both the location of the original natural progenitors, the location of the immediate parents and the location of any intermediate generations, e.g. Cmpt. K2 Elburgon, Kenya (immediate parents) ex Cmpt. 16 Nelspruit, South Africa ex Los Reyes, Hidalgo, Mexico (original natural forest progenitors), the practical forester will not worry as to which is, strictly, a provenance and which is not.

Over the last half century evidence has continually accumulated that, within a botanical species, significant genetic variation in forest trees is frequently associated with geographic differences between the places where they are growing. This is particularly the case where geographic displacement is associated with climatic or soil changes. Thus the word "provenance" is increasingly applied to areas characterized by the genetic nature of the populations growing there rather than their location alone, e.g. "The geographic source or location to which plants are native and within which their genetic characteristics have been developed through natural selection". For the purpose of seed collection, the ideal provenance, as described by researcher:

(a) Be composed of a community of potentially interbreeding trees of similar genetic constitution (and of significantly different genetic constitution from other provenances).

(b) Be sufficiently large for collection of reproductive material in quantities significant for forest practice.

(c) Be defined by means of boundaries, which can be identified in the field.

Although it is not yet possible, in most cases, to delineate the boundaries of natural provenances, there is ample evidence in many tropical as well as temperate species that significant genetic differences exist between them. In the case of derived provenances growing in plantations, boundaries can be defined much more easily and, after a generation or two of conscious selection by man, these "land races" often differ significantly from the original natural provenance.

Increasingly foresters recognise the vital importance of provenance and specify the precise provenance which they need to plant on a given site, not just the species. Even within a single country distinct provenances or races of a species are recognised; some may be morphologically distinct, others which look alike may differ in their adaptability to specific sites. A good example is the large number of provenances of Tectona grandis recognised in India. Seed collecting teams must therefore expect an increasing number of orders with a breakdown by provenance as well as species. This trend is to be encouraged but it does complicate collecting operations, since it is clearly more time-consuming to collect say 20 kg of seed from each of 10 different locations 100 km apart than to collect 200 kg in one area. Another difficulty is in deciding on the limits of a provenance. Often a provenance is named from the nearest village and there is no evidence to show whether there is a significant shift in gene frequencies in the populations 1 km, 10 km or 100 km away from the original collecting point. Some attempts have been made to define the limits of provenances or seed zones of a few north-temperate conifers and similar studies have been made more recently on the delineation of provenance regions of Pinus caribaea and P. oocarpa in Honduras. Provenance regions of Eucalyptus camaldulensis have been defined in terms of the main drainage systems in Australia but very little work has been done on this aspect in the tropical hardwoods. The need to collect more than one provenance of a species calls for increased care in planning field operations. Some widespread species flower and fruit a few weeks earlier at low than at high elevations and at lower than at higher latitudes. Knowledge of a species' phenological variation in relation to geography will assist the collector to choose the most appropriate sequence of collecting sites so as to extend the total duration of useful collections.

Stands

In contrast with provenances, the boundaries of individual stands are commonly well defined. In many cases the stands are being managed for seed production e.g. by thinning. Often they are in plantations. Seed orchards are a special case, designed for seed production before they are planted and managed continuously for that purpose. The problem with seed stands and seed orchards is thus not one of identification, bùt that their area may be insufficient to supply all the demands for seed placed on them. If this is likely to occur, it is advisable to require seed users to name second or third choices, in both stands and provenances, in case their full needs cannot be met from their first choice.

Determining Seed Quantities

Seed users need to define the quantity of seed needed of each species, provenance or stand. For this it is necessary to know the area of plantation to be established annually and the initial spacing to be used, together with an estimate of losses and culls in the nursery, of replacements needed after planting to achieve full stocking, and of the number of germinated seedlings to be expected from each kg of seed sown.

Information on planting area and initial spacing is usually available from Plantation Management Plans, while some guidance to germination rates is available in published documents (e.g. FAO 1975a). Whenever possible, local experience on variation between provenances and planting sites should be used to refine estimates based on average conditions. For example, seeds of two provenances of Picea abies weigh, respectively, 6 gm and 12 gm per 1000; seed of Eucalyptus cloeziana collected in the moist coastal forests of Queensland averages 100,000 – 400,000/kg, whereas seed from dry inland wood lands averages only 35,000 – 65,000/kg.

In Italy it was found that in nursery trials on several eucalypt species the number of plants produced as a percentage of viable seed ranged from 18 per cent for *E. robusta* to 46 per cent for *E. camaldulensis*. Similarly, differences in climate, soil and incidence of pests and diseases can have a big effect on the rate of losses in different nurseries and plantations, whether or not there are any differences in the efficiency of management. So it may be necessary to apply an appropriate "locality correction factor" or "nursery recovery factor" to arrive at an accurate estimate of seed requirements for a particular plantation project. Before sending in his final order for seed to a central seed unit or commercial seed merchant, the plantation project manager should deduct those quantities of seed already in stock or likely to be available by collection from older plantations within the project area.

Determining the Year for Seed Collection

Effect of Periodicity

Seed-bearing of many forest trees is rather irregular from year to year. One year with a heavy crop (a "seed year" or "mast year") may be followed by one or several years with a poor seed crop or none at all. This habit of periodicity in seeding is an important factor to consider when planning seed collecting operations. The collection of seeds in a good year confers a number of advantages. There can be a high intensity of selection of seed bearers, the cost of collection is lower, due to the concentration of the crop, and the seeds will usually be of higher germinative capacity and will retain their viability longer than those collected in a poor seed year. Damage from insects affects a smaller proportion of seeds in a good than in a bad seed year. A heavy seed crop usually reflects a previous heavy production of pollen, to which all or most trees in the stand have contributed. Collection in a good seed year therefore conserves a higher proportion of the genetic diversity among male parents than collection in a bad year which follows pollination from only a small number of trees.

Periodicity is well documented for many temperate conifers. For example on average *Pinus sylvestris* bears an abundant crop every 2-3 years and *Pseudotsuga menziesii* every 4-6 years in the UK. Since the period between the good crops is not regular, a general rule of collecting three years' sowing requirements whenever a species bears a heavy cone.

Periodicity in tropical species is less well documented. Irregular mast years in *Triplochiton* have a great influence on the regeneration, or lack of regeneration, of that species, although periodicity in pests and diseases (the weevil *Apion* and the fungal smut *Mycosyrinx*) may play as big a part in seed production as periodicity in flowering. Poor seed years have been recorded in *Pinus caribaea* and *P. oocarpa*, and *P. merkusii*. In other species periodicity is not marked. *Tectona grandis* has generally good flowering each year, although exceptionally good seed years are observed in some localities on a three or four year cycle. *Gmelina arborea* starts to seed early, from age 3 in the Philippines to age 7 in Nigeria and usually produces regular abundant crops but poor seed years have been recorded, at least in some provenances. *Pinus kesiya* bears abundant crops every year within its indigenous range and as an exotic if planted in the appropriate climate. *Cassia siamea*, *Acacia mearnsii*, *Cupressus lusitanica* and ornamentals such as *Delonix regia* and *Jacaranda mimosaefolia* are other species which can be expected to flower and fruit profusely each year. Periodicity may vary considerably between species within the same genus. Among eucalypts, *E. grandis*, *E. saligna* and *E. camaldulensis* usually bear heavy seed crops every two to three years, while *E. gomphocephala* and *E. maculata* only seed heavily at longer intervals. Dipterocarps in Malaysia have heavy seed years at unpredictable intervals of one to six years. Periodicity and flowering patterns of eucalypts can change when they are grown as exotics. *Eucalyptus maculata* and *E. citriodora* bear much larger crops more regularly when grown in plantations.

Even in good years, flowering may vary substantially from one locality to another. Sometimes individual trees of a stand are on different cycles, some flowering abundantly one year, others in the next.

Counting the Fruit Crop

For those species which are known to exhibit periodicity in flowering and fruiting, it is highly desirable to visit the stands to be collected well in advance of the fruiting season, in order to assess in which of them the next seed crop promises to be heavy enough to justify the cost of collection. Too little is known about which external factors have a decisive affect on flowering to allow prediction of future seed crops on the basis of climate. Estimation of the crop can best be done by counting flowers or young fruits on a sample of the trees in the collection stands. Assessment of the abundance of flowering can give a preliminary estimate of the potential seed crop, but may be misleading if there are subsequent severe losses e.g. from insects, wind or poor pollination. In *Eucalyptus regnans* trapping studies indicated that only about 15 per cent of flower buds and 30 per cent of flowers can be expected to develop into mature fruits. In species such as the pines, which take two years from pollination to ripen their fruits, a count of one year old cones can give a useful indication of the next year's crop, which can be confirmed by further inspection a month or two before collection is due to begin. Recurrent personal inspection of the future crop is the ideal and presents no problem if collection is carried out in seed orchards or easily accessible plantations or natural forest. It may be difficult or impossible for collecting teams working in inaccessible areas or for international expeditions working in several countries. In such cases the team leader may have to rely on reports from an experienced correspondent or on estimates made during the previous year's collections. If reliable local information is not available, a special reconnaissance may be justified in advance of the expensive collecting expedition.

Where the main seed collecting areas are located in less accessible places, it is useful to maintain permanent phenological plots in easily accessible locations within the same forest type, to act as biological indicators. Such plots should be monitored regularly so as to obtain a record of the timing and intensity of flowering and fruiting. The performance of the plots will indicate to collectors the best times to go into the less accessible areas of the district, to check for flowering. The boundaries of a phenological district that can be usefully served by a phenological plot must be defined by experience. In Malaysia, a sample of 86 Dipterocarp trees in an artificially established arboretum at the Forest Research Institute, Kepong, is monitored monthly or fortnightly and the percentage of trees flowering in a month or year is used as an index of Dipterocarp flowering for that month or year. This index gives a fairly reliable indication of Dipterocarp phenology within the State of Selangor (about 8000 sq. km) in which Kepong is located. Since the phenological plot in Kepong is within 10 minutes' walking distance from the researchers' offices and laboratories, a lot of time and money is saved which would otherwise have to be spent on transportation and organisation of field trips.

Where it is necessary to count the fruits or cones, binoculars or telescopes are an essential aid. They should be of high optical quality. In binoculars a wide field of view should be combined with only moderate magnification; a minimum of 50 mm aperture and magnification ×7 or ×8 are suitable. The normal method is to make counts on a representative sample of seed trees dispersed throughout the whole seed source. It is necessary to take the sample from within the stand, because the perimeter trees always fruit more heavily than the trees within the seed source. Counting may be done from the ground or by climbing neighbouring trees. Fruits are counted from one side of the crown only and the number counted is converted to an estimate of the total crop for that sample tree by a correction factor which varies according to the species and the abundance of the crop. In Czechoslovakia (counting from climbed trees) a factor 1.6 is used for Abies alba, which is constant irrespective of the size of crop, because the clustering of the cones near the top of the tree makes counting in this species reliable. For *Picea abies* the factor varies according to the average number of cones counted per tree; for 1-40 cones it is 1.4, for 41-70 cones it is 1.8 and for more than 70 cones it is 2.5. In the UK (counting from the ground) a factor of 4 is used for *Pinus*, *Larix* and *Pseudotsuga*, while for species with very numerous small cones the practice is to scan say one tenth of the crown from one side and use a factor of 20.

The number of sample trees used for cone counting varies according to the size of the stand. In the UK five trees are sampled in small seed sources less than 0.5 ha and the number increases progressively to 20 trees for seed sources of more than 4 ha. Czechoslovakia uses a series of plots, in each of which about 5 dominant trees are climbed to scan a further 10-15 neighbouring trees. In Tasmania extensive eucalypt seed sources are sampled at the rate of one tree per ha.

Fruit Crop Rating Methods

The results of cone or fruit counting are applied to the stand and expressed as a numerical value on a scale running from total crop failure to exceptional seed years. With experience it may be possible to define the criteria for an economically collectable crop in quantitative terms e.g. for *Pinus sylvestris* in the UK a minimum of 25 seed trees per ha each bearing at least 300-400 cones is specified. For conifers in Arizona and New Mexico researchers defined "Few" cones per tree as 1-20, "Many" as 21-160 and "Loaded" as over 160 cones per tree. Quantitative classifications of this type will clearly vary to a great extent according to species, provenance and site conditions.

More often use is made of qualitative scoring assessments which rely on the experience of the assessor. In Washington and Oregon (1982) five ratings are used, as shown below:

Rating Explanation

Other than true firs:

5 Heavy	–	Good crop of cones on all exposed crowns of most trees.
4 Medium	–	Good to medium crop on ¾ of exposed crown on most trees.
3 Light	–	Good to fair crop on ½ of exposed crown of ½ of trees.
2 Very light	–	Some cones on some trees.
1 Failure	–	No cones to a few scattered on a few trees.

True firs: (upper $S^3/_4$ of crown)

5 Heavy	–	Good crop of cones on most upper branches of most trees.
4 Medium	–	Good to medium crop on most trees.
3 Light	–	Few cones on many trees.
2 Very light	–	Few cones on scattered trees.
1 Failure	–	Nonexistent

A rating of 4 or 5 is good prospect for all pickers.
A rating of 3 has possibilities for more experienced pickers.
A rating of 1 or 2 is poor prospect for all pickers.

Each year the State Forest Service publishes estimated average cone crop ratings by species and geographic area, for the benefit of individual pickers. They are based on surveys of a number of different stands and the average for each area is expressed to one place of decimals. For example in 1972, a poor year, the best rating was 2.5 for *Tsuga heterophylla* in the Western Cascade of Oregon, while 1.0 or total failure was recorded for some species in more than one area.

In Tanzania a four class scale is used and seed crop estimates are made twice, one at flowering and the other about a month before seed collection. The classes are:

0 – *no seed crop.* Trees without flowers and fruits.

1 – *weak seed crop.* Flowering and medium size seed crop on free growing trees and trees on free borders of stands.

2 – *medium size seed crop.* Flowering and very good crop on free growing trees and on free borders of stands, trees within the stands bearing crop at the top of crowns.

3 – *very good seed crop.* Flowering and very good crop on most trees.

In Sweden forecasts of the cone and seed germinability of *Pinus sylvestris* and *Picea abies* have been made annually for about 80 years. Estimates are given separately for the different combinations of latitude (in 1° steps) and altitude (in 100 m steps).

Estimating Full Seed Content by Cutting Test

The methods described above provide an estimate of the cone or fruit crop. It is necessary to relate this to seed production by examining the contents of a sample of the fruit crop. Fruits may develop normally to maturity whether one or one hundred of the contained ovules have been successfully fertilized and undergone normal development; in parthenocarpous species fruits can mature without containing any sound seeds at all. The number of fruits is therefore not always a good guide to the number of seeds.

The method generally recommended is to cut cones or fruits lengthwise and count the number of seeds which can be seen on one cut surface. Special cone-cutting knives have been designed for this purpose. One or two cone samples from each of 20 to 100 trees in an area are suggested for southern pines in the USA, 5 or 10 cones from each of 10 trees in the UK. Only normal seeds should be counted.

Underdeveloped seeds which often occur at the top and base of cones are not included. The number of full seeds counted which denote a good crop varies according to species, for example 6 or more indicates a good crop in *Pseudotsuga*, 14 or more a good crop in *Picea sitchensis*. The relationship of the total number of full seeds per cone to number of full seeds exposed on a cut surface is known for some species, for example a factor of ×4 or ×5 is appropriate for *Pseudotsuga* in the western USA.

The average number of seeds per fruit for many tropical species is not known and needs to be established under local conditions; they vary from one seed per fruit in e.g. most Dipterocarps to several hundred per fruit in *Anthocephalus*. With multiseeded fruits, it is likely that the number of seeds developed will vary in accordance with climate, soil fertility and the age of the parent trees. The first crops borne by young trees nearly always contain fewer sound seeds per fruit than those borne by the same trees when fully mature.

Examination of a sample of seeds in the fruit serves the additional purposes of indicating the state of development or maturity of the seeds and the incidence of damage by pests or diseases.

Determining the Best Dates for Collection

Some species in the tropics carry some ripe seed at all times of the year. Even in these there is often a period of maximum seed production, when collection will be cheapest and seed quality highest. In other species, and especially in the temperate zone with its marked distinction between summer and winter, ripe seed is borne for a limited period, often during the autumn. For many species there is good information on average dates of the seeding season, but these averages may not be sufficiently accurate for planning collection in a particular year. The period between seed maturation and seed dispersal is often short, whereas the effects of climate in a given year may displace the dates of seeding by several weeks from the average. In the temperate zone an early spring and dry summer can cause very early seed ripening, while strong, dry winds cause rapid dispersal of the ripe seeds. Cool, wet weather, on the other hand may delay ripening and dispersal by weeks or months. In the dry tropics there are similar annual variations in the dates of the onset of the dry season and of the rains. It is therefore necessary in each year to check the correct timing of collection by examination of the crop itself.

The reconnaissance of the size of the seed crop, made 1-2 months before seed collection will also give some indications as to how the seeds are maturing. Conclusions from it should be two-fold e.g.: - "Stands A, B and C: Very light crops, not worth collecting this year. Stands X, Y, Z: Good crops, seeds probably mature in 4 weeks' time". A final check on the ripeness of seed must, however, be done at the time of collection.

The humid tropics present special problems because seasonality effects are usually subtle or absent and the period of maximum seed production is uncertain. After detection of flowering in a stand from which it is desired to collect seeds, it is important to carry out periodic reconnaissance to check on the progress of fruit maturation. An efficient schedule of reconnaissance requires prior knowledge of the length of time between anthesis (flower opening/pollination) and fruit maturity. Among Malaysian trees, the period from anthesis to fruit maturity varies from 3 weeks for *Pterocymbium javanicum* to 11 months for *Diospyros maingayi*. In the exotic Brazil nut, *Bertholletia excelsa*, the period is 15-16 months. In Malaysia it is recommended that if the maturation period is × weeks, the development of the crop should be checked at ½ × and 3/4 × weeks after flowering. A fixed and arbitrary schedule of, say, once a month, will result in the collector being too late for a fast-maturing fruit like *Pterocymbium javanicum* and too wasteful of effort in the case of a slow-maturing fruit like the Brazil nut.

Apart from the exceptional case of deliberate collection of immature seeds, seed collectors need to be able to time collection for the period when seeds (but not necessarily fruits) are fully ripe but before they are dispersed by fruit dehiscence or fruit consumption by animals. To achieve this aim collectors must be able to distinguish ripe from unripe seeds. Several different methods have been used for the recognition of seed maturity. None of them work perfectly on all species and a good deal of experience or research is needed to determine the best method, or combination of methods, for a hitherto unfamiliar species. They may be divided into those which are of direct application in the field and those which need laboratory equipment. The latter may be valuable in providing a check on the field methods, but are unlikely to be of practical use to the collector unless the collection site happens to be close to the laboratory, which may be the case for some seed orchards.

Laboratory Methods

(a) **Dry weight:** The most generally accepted measure of maturity is the time when the seed has reached its maximum dry weight, a point called physiological maturity. This means that nutrients are no longer flowing into the seed from the mother tree. Maximum fresh weight does not indicate physiological maturity because the maturing seed begins losing water while nutrients are still being accumulated and biochemical processes are continuing.

Recurrent dry-weight determination of a series of seed samples can be made and the results extrapolated to the remaining crop, but this method is slow and therefore seldom used.

(b) **Chemical analysis:** Biochemical changes take place as seeds mature but relatively little is known for most species. Chemical indices of seed maturity have been determined in a few species e.g. content of crude fat and protein-nitrogen, which increase five and four times respectively from immaturity to physiological maturity, are the best chemical indices for *Fraxinus pennsylvanica*.

But they have no advantages over an examination of the embryo and the colour change of the fruit, and the extra trouble to perfom the analyses does not appear to be justified. Researcher found that *Pseudotsuga* seeds were physiologically mature when the content of reducing sugars dropped to 14 mg/g.

(c) **X-ray radiography:** The examination of the development of the embryo and endosperm of sample seeds by means of X-ray radiographs is a quick and relatively straightforward method of assessing seed maturity, provided that suitable facilities and skilled technical staff are available. The technique has been used successfully for *Tectona* and a number of other tropical species, as well as for temperate species such as *Pinus strobus*. It has the disadvantage of requiring relatively expensive equipment and relies heavily on the judgment of the seed analyst for reliable results.

(d) **Moisture content of fruits:** Water loss of maturing cones and fruits occurs in many species and is closely related to the maturity of the seed. Seeds of *Picea glauca* are considered ripe when moisture content falls below 48 per cent, of *Larix decidua* at 25-30 per cent and of *Pinus sylvestris* when it falls to 43-45 per cent (fresh weight basis). However, determination of moisture content by drying in an oven suffers the same disadvantage of slowness as determination of dry weight.

Field Methods

(e) **Specific gravity of fruits:** As moisture content of fruits and cones decreases with maturation, so does specific gravity or density, the ratio of unit weight to unit volume, decrease. Unlike moisture content, it is not too difficult to determine approximate specific gravity in the field by flotation in liquids of known specific gravity. Specific gravity indices of maturity have been established for cones of a number of coniferous species, and the cone to be tested is placed in a liquid in which it will float if mature and sink if immature. Various mixtures of kerosene (SG = 0.80), light SAE 20 motor oil (SG = 0.88) and linseed oil (SG = 0.93) have been used to prepare flotation liquids having a designated specific gravity. Tests must be made immediately after cones are picked from a tree. Specific gravity indices have proved reliable for some temperate conifers e.g. an S.G. of 0.74 for *Picea glauca* (Cram and Worden 1957), but not for several southern hardwoods in the USA.

(f) **Examination of seed contents:** Examination of seed contents exposed by cutting open fruits or cones lengthwise can be a reliable and simple method of assessing seed ripeness, provided the operator is experienced. Most embryos and endosperm pass through an immature "milk" stage, followed by a "dough" stage when the tissue becomes more firm. Mature seeds have a firm white endosperm (where present) and a fully developed firm embryo.

(g) **Colour of fruits or cones:** Colour changes in fruit or cone provide a simple and, in some species, reliable criterion for judging seed maturity, but the operator must be experienced in the characteristics of the species concerned. In common with the specific gravity method, it involves no destruction of the seeds in the sample examined. Colour changes are usually from the green of the immature fruit or cone to various shades of yellow, brown or grey, and this may be accompanied by hardening of cone scales or of the pericarp of dehiscent or woody fruits. Since the seed normally matures before the fruit, it is advisable in some species to time collection at an earlier rather than a later stage of the colour change. Colour change was found to be the most reliable indicator of maturity for general practice in several southern hardwoods in the USA. It has also given good results in a number of temperate conifers. In Malaysia researcher found that the best results were obtained by timing collection of Dipterocarp fruits when the wings turned brown but before the fruit itself changed colour.

In Thailand cone colour is used as a guide to optimum time of collection of pines, but differs according to species. In *Pinus kesiya* collection starts when cones have hardened and the colour is changing from green to brown in proportions of 50 : 50. In *Pinus merkusii* optimum time of collection is reached when the majority of cones are brownish and some have started to open. Trials with the Zambales (Philippines) provenance of *P. merkusii* have shown not only that extraction is a much more lengthy and expensive operation with green than with brown cones but also that the seed extracted has lower germination rate. Experience with *P. caribaea* in Honduras is similar.

Abscission and shedding of fruits is usually a sign of fruit maturity and it might be assumed that it also indicates a high content of sound, mature seeds. This is not always the case. The first seeds or fruits which fall naturally are often of poor quality, in which case it is advisable to reject them and to postpone collection until the peak and the latter half of the season. In Thailand fruits of *Tectona grandis* start to be shed in March but observations have shown that the most viable fruits are the last to be shed, so collection starting only in April is recommended. The first fruits of Dipterocarp species that fall upon ripening are usually defective and collecting should be delayed until the greater portion of the fruit has fallen.

Collection of Immature Seeds

It is general practice to collect seeds when they are mature, because they have a higher germinative energy and a greater longevity in storage than immature seeds. An alternative method is to collect fruits prior to ripening and to store them in relatively cool, well ventilated conditions which permit afterripening of the seeds within the fruit. It has shown promise on a research scale in a number of species.

There are several reasons for the interest in developing techniques for artificial ripening. They are:

- *To extend the collection season:* The short period between seed maturity and dispersal may place an excessive demand on the availability of seasonal labour and in some areas unfavourable weather conditions in the collection period may aggravate this situation. Lengthening the period available for collection permits better organisation of the collections and allows skilled personnel to pick more of the crop. It can be particularly valuable in research, where a large number of seed lots have to be collected from widely scattered localities. researcher used the technique in his study of Douglas fir provenances.
- *To avoid damage to the seed crop by insects and other pests:* Insects, birds, rodents and other pests frequently damage or destroy seeds and fruits when they have reached maturity. Early collection may be one method of avoiding these losses. Damage and deterioration of seeds is usually worse during the period while they lie on the forest floor than during any other stage in their history; any reduction in this period will improve their subsequent viability and longevity in storage.
- *To salvage immature seed collected inadvertently:* Untrained collectors of seeds often begin picking fruits and cones too early in the year before they are fully mature. Artificial ripening provides a method for handling this material.

The development of techniques for after-ripening of immature seeds will require more research, before they can be applied to a wide range of species. However, where a problem of rapid dispersal or of seed pests exists and provided the earliest time for safe collection of immature fruits can be established, such techniques can be very beneficial.

Determining which Trees to Collect From

If it can be assumed that the seed collector has received clear directions from the seed user as to which species and provenances and, in some cases, from which stands he is to collect, it is still his responsibility to select the individual trees for collection. Criteria will vary considerably according to whether the collections are large-scale for afforestation projects or small-scale for research purposes.

Identification of species presents no problems in monospecific plantations, but is essential and may be difficult in mixed natural forest, especially where very similar species of the same genus occur mixed together as happens with pines in Mexico and Central America, eucalypts in Australia and dipterocarps in S.E. Asia. Unless identification is certain, it is often advisable to collect herbarium specimens as well as seed.

Large-scale Collections

In large-scale collections emphasis is on collecting as much seed as possible, as quickly and cheaply as possible, rather than on very careful selection of the parent trees. It is, nevertheless, essential to avoid collecting seeds from very poor phenotypes or seeds which prove to be empty or non-viable. Useful guidelines are listed following:

1. Collect seed only from healthy vigorous trees of reasonably good form that are making average or better growth.
2. Where possible, collect from mature or nearly mature trees. Overmature trees should be avoided, since seeds from them may be of low viability.
3. Avoid isolated trees of naturally cross-pollinating species, since these are likely to be self-pollinated. Seeds are likely to be few, of low viability, and any seedlings produced are frequently weak or malformed.
4. Avoid collecting in stands containing numerous poorly formed, excessively limby, off-colour, abnormal or diseased trees.

Often it will be necessary to compromise between seed production and phenotypic appearence. No seed should be collected from excessively coarse-branched, vigorous “wolf” trees, even though they often bear a large crop, while trees of exceptionally good form sometimes bear so little seed that they do not warrant the trouble of collection. The bulk of seed will come from trees which are "average or better than average" in both form and seed production.

Although few studies have been made of the reproductive biology of tropical trees, the occurrence of some species at a very low stocking (less than one every km^2) suggests that these must be naturally self-pollinated. Seed collection from such trees is free from disadvantages associated with collections from isolated trees of natural cross-pollinators.

Small-scale Research Collections

In small-scale collections for research, selection of trees will depend on the precise objective of the planned research. Provenance research is now receiving a good deal of attention in many countries. Advice of IUFRO on provenance seed collections includes the following recommendations on collections from individual trees:

1. Collect from not worse than dominant and co-dominant trees of average quality, within "normal" rather than "plus" stands. Collections from superior phenotypes, if made, should be kept separately.
2. Collect from a minimum of 10 trees, preferably from 25 to 50 in the stand. If the stand is very variable, increase the number of trees. Record the number of trees and the approximate percentage which they form of the stand.
3. Seed trees to be at least seed fall distance apart from each other. A distance of 100 m has been adopted for *Pseudotsuga*. This is to reduce the risk of collecting from half-sib parents. In Australia a minimum distance of twice tree height is used as a practical rule of thumb.
4. Individual seed trees to be marked.
5. Collect equal numbers of cones, fruits or seeds per tree.

6. In normal first stage provenance collections, seed from individual trees may be mixed together. If special studies on individual genotypes are to be done, seed from each tree should be kept separate.

Single Tree Collections

Foresters are interested in the variation within populations and provenance as well as the variation between them. In the case of exotics, one approach for the introducing countries is to study between provenance differences under local conditions first, and to investigate variation between individuals in the best provenance, by means of progeny trials, only at a later stage after the provenances locally best adapted have been identified. If progeny trials are the object of seed collection, it is essential to keep seed from individual trees separate at all stages of collection, transport, processing, nursery and field planting.

The preservation of the identity of individual trees through the collection and extraction phase often requires considerably more effort than bulking the collections. If the effort is made, then certain advantages accrue:

- It permits biosystematic study of genetic variation both within and between populations. Researcher states that seed collections must be kept separate by individual trees throughout the test from collection to outplanting, as provenance tests are weakened by combining seed within a stand, making it impossible to distinguish between seed source and individual variation. However, in large provenance tests with many individual trees, it may be beyond the resources of the investigator to retain the identity of the parents.
- It is possible to manipulate to equalize the amount of viable seed from each tree in the provenance mix if the seed must be bulked prior to sowing.
- It is not always possible to detect trees bearing hybrid seeds in the field. This is particularly the case with

eucalypts. If seedlots are kept separate then, following the raising of small samples from each tree, any showing evidence of hybridization can be eliminated before the main trial is established.

Single Clone Collections

In seed collection in clonal seed orchards, the unit of identity to be kept separate is often the clone rather than the individual ramet. In Zimbabwe the practice of keeping individual clonal seedlots separate has been followed for many years and it is considered that it more than justifies the additional costs and efforts involved over bulked orchard collections. The advantages can be summarized as follows:

(a) Maintaining individual clonal identities at all stages from collections through to storage enables one to act with the minimum of delay on most information as it becomes available. The more obvious areas where action can be taken quickly are when rogueing becomes necessary or when susceptibility to pests or diseases becomes apparent, and the undesirable seedlots can be isolated or discarded.

(b) Seedlots can be made up and supplied to suit specific sites, making use of the most recent information on genotype/environment interaction from progeny test analyses.

(c) In conjunction with (b) above, and using the test results of each clone, composite seedlots can be made up in such a way as to give equal clonal representation in the final planting stock, avoiding the dominating effects that some clones frequently have in a bulked seedlot.

(d) In general, it increases the options available to the user.

Collections for Conservation

Collections are also made for the purpose of attempting to conserve the gene pool *ex situ* either as seed in long-term storage or in planted conservation stands. Because exact knowledge of gene frequencies in the indigenous populations is largely lacking, collecting for gene conservation must be based mainly on commonsense. Similar methods as for provenance collections are likely to be appropriate, with the exceptions that:

1. A somewhat larger number of trees per genepool should be sampled. Estimates are in the range or 50 to 100.
2. The sample should be a strictly random one and include poorer than average as well as better than average trees, in order to capture as much as possible of the total genetic variation. The only restriction on this principle is the impossibility of sampling trees which are bearing no seed.
3. An additional measure to ensure the fullest possible genetic diversity within the seed collected is to collect in a better than average seed year. The better the seed year, the better the representation of male parents contributing pollen as well as of female parents supplying seed.
4. The quantity of seed to be collected from each provenance will usually be larger, because the recommended area for a conservation stand, 10 ha, is much greater than the total area of one provenance in a single provenance trial.

Assembling Resources for Seed Collection

One part of planning is the timely assembly of clear information on the nature and magnitude of the seed collection tasks - number of species and provenances, seed quantities, location of stands, best dates to collect etc., as described above. The other part is to select and assemble the resources needed to do the job. Details of the various resources which may be useful are discussed in subsequent chapters. During the planning stage, the leader of collecting operations needs to check the preparations for field work under the following headings:

1. *Organisation of collecting teams:* Known or estimated output of collecting teams needs to be related to the quantity of seed, number of stands and length of season,

in order to determine the required number and size of teams. For example provenance collections of *Pinus kesiya* totalling 3000 kg of cones from 16 stands can be completed in 30 days by one team in Thailand. If the full season is estimated at 45 days and there is a demand for a total at 9000 kg of cones from the same 16 stands, two teams will be needed to do the job. If planning can be done sufficiently in advance, it may give an opportunity to train additional climbers if they are needed. It is desirable to have at least one tree-climber on the permanent staff, who can be responsible for looking after climbing equipment and for training new temporary climbers. In the field the climbers should be organized in small teams with a foreman in charge of each. In Honduras a team of 6 pairs (with one climber and one ground assistant or anchorman in each pair) has been found to be a suitable size.

2. *Organisation of transport:* Collecting teams need to cut to a minimum the time spent in moving between one site and the next. Transport must be available where and when it is needed. If necessary, extra vehicles may be temporarily hired. In roadless country, advance arrangements may be needed to employ extra unskilled workers to assist in carrying equipment, tents, etc.
3. *Organisation of equipment:* Choice of equipment will vary greatly according to local conditions. The steeper and less accessible the terrain, the simpler and lighter should be the equipment. Whereas highly mechanised equipment such as tree shakers or mechanised platforms may be appropriate in large seed orchards on flat land, only light portable equipment is practical where natural stands are 4-6 hours' walk from the nearest road. Apart from collecting tools, safety clothing, first aid equipment and plenty of bags and sacks should be provided.
4. *Organisation of records:* Meticulous recording and labelling is essential to good collecting. Appropriate labels and forms need to be designed well in advance and printed in adequate numbers.

5. *Organisation of permits:* These are not normally required for forest services collecting in government forest reserves, but may be needed when collecting on private land, in National Parks and special reserves, or in another country. Even if formal authority is not needed, it is often advisable to inform local communities of proposed operations in advance.
6. *Organisation of seed extraction:* Arrangements for rapid movement of fruits from collection site to extractory may be needed, involving the advance organisation of transport. The seed extractory staff must be advised when to expect the fruits. If some preliminary sun-drying of fruits in the forest is planned, polythene sheeting or tarpaulins will be needed.

Special Considerations for International Expeditions

Some species are currently of greater importance as plantation trees in exotic situations than they are in the source countries. Examples are *Gmelina arborea*, *Pinus radiata*, many sub-tropical and tropical pines and many eucalypts. When the natural range of such species extends through several different countries and the seed is in demand by many introducing countries, international action may be the most effective way of organising collection and distribution of seed. This is particularly true in the case of collections for provenance trials and for the establishment of *ex situ* conservation stands, seed stands and pilot plantations, for which only small or moderate quantities of seed are needed but sources must be precisely identified and fully documented. Examples of international collections of this type are those organised by IUFRO for western North American conifers, by CFI Oxford for Central American pines and hardwoods and by the DANIDA Forest Seed Centre for *Tectona* and *Gmelina.*

Researcher has described those problems in seed collection which are accentuated in the international context. These include especially the difficulty of obtaining accurate information in advance, on which to base the detailed plan of operations, and problems concerned with crossing international borders, customs regulations, language differences and so on. There are many uncertainties regarding access, travel and transport of material which may only be resolved when the collection is actually in progress. This is particularly true in many tropical countries, in which precise information on the natural distribution, variability, flowering and fruiting times, etc. of the species concerned may be incomplete or entirely lacking. While this makes precise planning of operations more difficult, it also calls for long and careful consideration of the many possible situations that may be actually encountered and the preparation of contingency plans to meet such situations, as well as to allow for unknown emergencies that may arise. Some particular aspects which must be considered in international expeditions are briefly stated below.

1. *Objectives:* Because an international expedition is likely to be undertaken on behalf of many countries, it may be attempting to meet several different objectives at the same time, such as collection of seed for provenance trials, bulk seed for large plantations of selected sources, collection from individual phenotypes and so on. Expeditions involving a lengthy period of travel in distant areas are very expensive and must therefore be used as fully as possible to meet different needs, but nevertheless these needs may to some extent conflict. Since the time available for collection is always limited, a choice may have to be made between spending longer at an individual site, for detailed sampling or bulk collection, and covering more sites more quickly. For this reason, the objectives must be clearly defined in advance and an order of priority established in case it is necessary to choose between them.
2. *Local Regulations:* Most countries have regulations governing collection, export, introduction and perhaps movement of seed. Official permits may be required for

any of these procedures and failure to obtain the necessary documents may seriously delay current operations as well as jeopardizing future collecting by international teams. Similarly the expedition staff may require personal documents, such as entry visas, work permits and international health certificates. Some equipment may also be subject to importation restrictions, particularly firearms and, perhaps "walkie-talkie" radios, if these are to be used.

3. *Involvement of local staff:* International expeditions can benefit enormously from the active involvement of local personnel. They can assist in interpretation and their knowledge of local geography and customs can be extremely valuable. They may also be in a position to reconnoitre seed crops in advance of further collections in subsequent years. In return, arrangements may be made for travel expenses of local personnel to be borne by international funds and for the host country to receive a part of the seed collected. Such arrangements should be agreed on both sides in advance.
4. *Equipment:* Decisions on the most appropriate equipment to use, and the essential items to be supplied to the expedition in advance, are more difficult without previous knowledge of the area and local conditions. Transport of bulky equipment by air is expensive, but equally a delay in the start of operations once the expedition is in the field, due to lack of needed equipment, can be very costly of both funds and the limited time available for collection.
5. *Timing of operations:* It is preferable to collect only in a year of abundant seed production, since this offers much greater freedom of action in the choice of stands and trees, as well as the possibility of obtaining more seed for a given cost. However, international expeditions must be prepared far in advance of the time when crop assessment is possible and the complex arrangements

involved make it very difficult to alter plans at a late stage. Even in a year of abundant seed production, best results can only be achieved if the actual season for collection is accurately known, and this is more difficult for an international expedition, based elsewhere, to determine in advance.

6. *Field Records:* Because of the difficulty and high cost of obtaining data once the expedition has left the area, particularly if it might involve returning there to make fresh observations, accurate and full records of the sites and collection details are most important.

Seed Collection

Introduction

present chapter describes the various methods available, both manual and mechanical, for the actual operation of collecting seed from a given tree. Although the term "seed collection" is a convenient one in common use, it should be noted that almost invariably it is the fruits which are harvested from the trees. Only at a later stage in some species are the seeds extracted and the fruits discarded; in other species seed extraction is omitted and fruits are sown in the nursery complete with the one or more seeds which they contain.

There is a great variety of methods and equipment available for collection of fruits and the choice depends on a number of factors which, may be summarized as follows:

1. Relative size and numbers of the natural dispersal units and of the units which can be conveniently collected by man. In the case of 1-3 large seeds inside a dehiscent or indehiscent fruit (e.g. *Aesculus*, *Tectona*), collection can be done most easily by awaiting natural fall of seed or fruit and collecting from the ground. At the other extreme collection from the tree of fruiting heads of *Adina cordifolia* at 200 per kg is the only practicable way to collect the seeds; at 11 million per kg, it would be impossible to collect them after dispersal.

2. *Characteristics of the fruit:* size, number, position and distribution of fruits; resistance of peduncles to shaking, pulling, breaking or cutting; interval between ripening and opening.
3. *Characteristics of the tree:* diametre, shape and length of bole, bark thickness; shape of crown; size, angle, density and resistance to breakage of branches; density of foliage and depth of crown.
4. *Characteristics of the stand:* distribution and stocking of trees (e.g. isolated trees, open or dense stand); density of understorey and ground vegetation).
5. *Characteristics of the site:* slope, accessibility.

The various collection methods may be classified into the following:

(a) Collection of fallen fruits or seeds from the forest floor;
(b) Collection from the crowns of felled trees;
(c) Collection from standing trees with access from the ground;
(d) Collection from standing trees with access by climbing; and
(e) Collection from standing trees with other means of access.

Collection of Fallen Fruits or Seeds from the Forest Floor

Natural Seedfall

Collection from the forest floor of fruits which have fallen after natural ripening and abscission is common practice with a number of large-fruited genera. It is cheap and does not require as highly skilled labour as, for example, climbing; school children or casual labour may be used. Fruit size is very important as the larger the fruit, the easier it is to see and pick up by hand. Temperate genera commonly collected from the ground are *Quercus*, *Fagus*, *Castanea* and tropical genera include *Tectona*, *Gmelina*, *Triplochiton* and several genera among the dipterocarps.

The main disadvantages of collection from natural fruit shedding are the risks of collecting immature, empty or unsound seeds, of seed deterioration or premature germination if collection is delayed, and uncertainty in identifying the mother trees from which seed is collected. Seeds in the first fruits to fall naturally in the season are often of poor quality. In Thailand shedding of teak fruits starts in March, but observations have shown that the most viable fruits are shed in the latter part of the season, so collection is usually postponed until April. Clearing the forest floor of vegetation and debris, including old or prematurely fallen fruits, and/or spreading out sheeting of light canvas, calico or plastic, to catch the seed, can greatly facilitate collecting efficiency. If carefully timed, this operation will also eliminate much of the risk of collecting empty or non-viable seed. Sound fruits should be gathered as soon as possible after they have fallen, to avoid damage or losses from insects, rodents or fungi and premature germination. This is of particular importance in the moist tropical forest. Observations have indicated that many of the seeds of the more important dipterocarps lose their viability within a few days of shedding and studies on *Shorea platyclados* in Malaysia demonstrated that seed lots collected from the ground included considerably more defective seeds than lots collected from the standing tree. Collection from the ground must, therefore, be perfectly timed with seedfall.

In the Jari region of Amazonia in Brazil, researchers found that collection of green or yellow fruits of *Gmelina arborea* from the forest floor gave the best results in operations for collecting about 10,000 kg of seed a year. They could be stored temporarily in sacks during transit from the field to the fruit processing depot, without serious loss of viability. Older brown or black fruits ferment and heat in the sacks and rapidly lose viability. Collecting teams are instructed to collect only the fresh green and yellow fruits. 50 kg of fruits can be collected per man in an 8 hour working day and yield about 3 kg of dried stones. Similar results have been obtained in Malaysia where green and yellow fruits collected from the ground gave over 90 per cent germination, but brown fruits, on the other hand, produced only 53 per cent.

Seeds of some hard-coated species may remain viable on the forest floor for years, especially in temperate conditions. In Hungary seed of *Robinia pseudoacacia* is collected from the forest floor under 30-year-old stands in the Pusztavacs forest district. A special machine screens the top 10 cm of soil and yields about 770 kg of seed per hectare, which is the equivalent of the yield of approximately 10 seed years. Even in the tropics viable hard-coated seeds may be obtained by screening the soil below the mother trees. This has been done in Malaysia for *Parkia javanica* and *Intsia palembanica* of which the seeds are large enough to be picked up by hand. Where the seeds are smaller e.g. in *Albizzia falcataria*, sieving with a wire mesh may be more practical.

The identity of the mother tree is often uncertain when fruits are collected from the ground. Isolated trees present no problem in this respect (though they may be undesirable parents because of the risk of selfing), but much mixing of fruits can occur in dense monocultures with interlocking crowns. This is of no concern in collecting commercial quantities of seed, provided that the genetic quality of the stand is average or above average. For research and breeding purposes, it is often necessary to maintain the identity of the mother tree of each seed lot. In such cases it is advisable to clear the grond of already fallen fruits and to accelerate the fall of new fruits by shaking, beating or cutting off branches, or climbing and picking fruits in the crown. A compromise solution, suitable for commercial collections in unimproved stands containing a mixture of good and bad phenotypic trees, is to collect fruits only below the better seed bearers and within half the radius of projection of their crowns.

Manual Shaking

If fruits are easily detached but natural fruit fall is insufficiently concentrated in time, fruit fall may be induced by artificial means. Trunks of small trees and low branches may be shaken directly by hand. Higher branches may be shaken by means of a long pole and hook or by a rope. This method has produced good results in *Cordia alliodora* and *Cedrela* spp., as it facilitates rapid collection of seed with good viability as soon as visual inspection shows that the fruits are mature.

Use of a rope involves an initial operation to pass the rope over the branch to be shaken, which is described by the researchers. The same method is used to hoist a saw or pulley into the crown. A thin line is attached to a weight, which is projected over the branch by hand or by catapult. For higher branches the line may be attached to an arrow, which is shot from a bow, or to an iron rod shot from a calibre .22 rifle. A light nylon line such as a fishing line of 50 lbs. (23 kg) breaking strain is suitable and the weight or projectile used should be heavy enough to drop to the ground pulling the line with it over the branch. Care must be taken to ensure that the line unreels readily without getting entangled, for example by using an appropriate fishing reel. Once the end of the line has reached the ground, the weight or arrow can be detached and a nylon cord of 3-4 mm attached instead; the line is drawn back over the branch, pulling the cord with it. The two ends of the loop can then be pulled together to shake the branch. The cord should be positioned towards the end of the branch where it will have the maximum shaking effect and not close to the bole where the branch is thickest.

In New Zealand a 30 kg-pull fibreglass long-bow firing arrows 0.8-0.9 m long and 40 g in weight has been used to project a line of 5.5 kg breaking strain over a branch. This is used, successively, to pull up a 20 kg line and a 180 kg line with pulley. In Canada both a .45 calibre gun firing a steel rod of 270 g weight and a .22 calibre gun firing a cylinder of 230-300 g weight and 2½ inch diameter have been used successfully up to heights varying from 20-50 m. Blank cartridges were used. The line attached to the projectile was

32 kg monofilament fishing line, which was used to haul up a 320 kg plastic twine carrying a branch breaking or cutting device.

Mechanical Shaking

Mechanical tree shakers were developed originally for fruit and nut orchards but since about 1965 the technique has been used for certain forest trees, particularly for the southern pines in the USA. The machines are expensive, need flat ground for efficient use, and experienced operators are essential to avoid excessive damage to the trees. Many cones are removed by a few seconds of shaking, but longer shaking breaks off pieces of tops and limbs. Tree shakers have no role in diffuse collecting operations in natural forest, but will probably continue to be used in intensively managed seed orchards or seed stands of a limited range of species.

The American Shock Wave tree shaker is mounted on a short wheel base truck chassis, equipped with an automatic transmission. It has a padded clamping device mounted on the extreme end of a 6 metre boom capable of clamping the trunk of a tree up to 90 cm diameter. A shake pattern is developed by counterrotation unbalanced weights in the shaker of varying frequency from 400-4000 cycles per minute.

The tree is generally clamped about 3 m above the ground and one 15-second shake is sufficient to remove about 80 per cent of the cones from *P. elliottii*; but *P. taeda* and *P. echinata* are more difficult and a good operator may often remove only 25-30 per cent of the cones after prolonged shaking. Ripe *P. elliottii* cones require a force of about 2 kg for removal whereas *P. taeda* cones are detached only by a force of 20 kg or more. An unsuccessful attempt to reduce the force needed to remove the cones of *P. taeda* by the use of abscission inducing chemicals is reported. The repeated shaking of the more difficult trees can cause bark rupture and breakage of the leading shoot.

With five mechanical shakers the Louisiana Forestry Commission harvested cones from 34,680 *P. elliottii* trees in twenty days. Three-quarters of the trees released 85 per cent of their cones during shaking periods from 6-30 seconds. Performance in one hour exceeded that of a climber in a week. Results showed that the mechanical shaking of Pinus elliottii trees by trained operators did not harm future cone production, tree growth or vigour over the following four years.

Mechanical tree shakers are now widely used in the southeastern USA for harvesting seed in seed orchards of pines. In the case of species in which ripe cones can be easily detached, such as *P. elliottii* and *P. palustris*, trees are shaken in the period after cones have reached maturity but before they open, and the cones with their contained seeds are collected from the ground. In the case of species with persistent cones, such as *P. taeda* and *P. echinata*, shaking is deferred until the cones have opened and the objective is to shake out the seeds from the cones. They can then be collected from the ground by means of the net retrieval system.

In the U.S.S.R. output from the VUS-2 vibrator working on *Pinus sibirica* was reported to be 10-20 times that obtained by manual methods. More recent experience with a tree-shaking machine developed in Soviet Central Asia has shown that 90-100 per cent of fruits of *Juglans*, *Malus*, *Prunus*, *Fraxinus* and *Gleditsia* can be collected with little stem damage. The machine is a grab-type vibrator mounted on a hydraulically operated arm on the 3-point linkage of a tractor. Optimum shaking time is 10-25 seconds and optimum vibration rate for most species 1000 cycles per minute. Italian CECMA vibrator machines, developed primarily for harvesting the olive crop, have also been used successfully for collecting cones of Mediterranean pines.

Collection of Seed after Dispersal

Although collection from the ground is most often used for fruits, it can also be used for seeds dispersed after the cones or fruits have opened. The seeds of southern pines in the USA, e.g. *Pinus elliottii* and *P. taeda* have a very short period between reaching maturity and being dispersed, and a number of methods have been evaluated for collecting loose seeds as they are dispersed. In addition to the use of sheeting spread on the ground, mentioned previously, they they include polypropylene netting round the crowns, funnel-shaped wooden frames covered with cloth or polyethylene and attached to a central hub surrounding the stem, and sheeting or nets raised on poles above the ground. Earlier experience was not very successful, as rarely more than 50 per cent of the available seed crop was recovered. If seed is borne mainly on or near the outside of the crown, much of it falls outside the spread of a single tree catching unit. If sheeting or netting must remain in place for an extended period of natural seed fall, it is liable to get damaged from weather and a proportion of the seeds are lost to birds and animals.

More recently a net retrieval system, for use in seed orchards in southern USA, has been developed jointly by the Georgia Forestry Commission and the Missoula Equipment Development Centre. It shows considerable promise and is increasingly preferred to vacuum harvesters in *P. taeda* orchards. Netting used is a polypropylene plastic fabric manufactured for carpet backing. It is light, durable and available in a range of dimensions. For *Pinus taeda* a width of 16.5 ft (5m) and a weave count of 6 × 8 per square inch (approximately 2 × 3 per cm^2) is used. If carefully handled, the expected life is 10+ years. Netting is laid in the orchard several weeks before seed fall and trees are shaken by mechanical shaker to dislodge seeds from the cones. The power take off from a wheeled tractor provides the power (less the 30 h.p.) needed for:

(a) Mechanical winding of the net onto a roller; and

(b) Mechanical separation of seed from the twigs, leaves and cones which also fall to the ground as a result of the shaking operation. Care must be taken in separating the netting from the grass blades which tend to go through it, before starting to wind in the netting.

Gathering of fruits on the ground is usually done manually but may be assisted by using a simple hand tool, such as a long-handled rake with interchangeable heads having different numbers of, and spacing between, tines. Attempts have been made to develop mechanical or vacuum sweeper methods to pick up seeds or fruits. Tests have also been made of a mechanical harvester, with the sweeping action of a rotating drum fitted with a myriad of attached rubber fingers which pick up seeds with separation from foreign debris. These types of machine are best used in conjunction with a tree shaker, which ensures that a substantial quantity of seeds are on the ground at each sweeping operation.

Researcher described the successful use in France of a vacuum sweeper type of machine, operated by compression from a tractor engine, for collection of *Fagus* fruits. The machine is compact and weighs 450 kg. A Dutch vacuum seed harvester has been used successfully for the collection of *Quercus* acorns and is reported to be a cheaper method in the Netherlands than either hand-picking or the use of a tree shaker and tarpaulins.

In the USA, researcher summarized the advantages of the vacuum sweeper as: it

1. Extends the harvesting season from about 2 weeks to 2 months.
2. Eliminates the need for ladders and lift trucks, permitting orchard managers to let their trees grow taller because no climbing is involved, therefore extending the useful life of the trees.
3. Reduces collection costs compared to hand collection.

The disadvantages of the harvester are that:

1. The orchard floor requires extensive preparation for the machine to operate well.
2. The harvester is noisy and produces large quantities of dust.

3. It does not operate well when the ground is wet.
4. The harvester has had a number of mechanical problems that have been largely corrected, but minor design changes still need to be made.

The disadvantages are now considered to outweigh the advantages, and the net retrieval system is preferred for collecting *P. taeda* seeds in orchards in the southern USA.

In view of the capital cost of this type of equipment and the emphasis placed on the immaculate preparation of the seed orchard floor which is needed for its operation, its use in developing countries is likely, especially if social considerations favour the use of labour-intensive manual methods as a means of increasing employment.

Animal Caches

Animals sometimes gather together cones or fruits as a food supply and these caches may be raided for the seed, but this source of seeds is confined to limited areas. Squirrel caches are an important source of coniferous seed in western North America. Squirrels usually locate their caches year after year in the same places. Typically, they are found in damp areas near springs, small creeks or marshes, on northern exposures, and in decayed wood or duff or around old fallen trees. A single cache may contain from a few cones to many bushels. Fresh cones on the ground are a sign of squirrel activity; piles of cone scales and cores may indicate a nearby cache. Caution should be exercised in collecting seeds or cones from caches, because of the danger of infestation by pathogenic fungi which may reduce germination.

Ants sometimes gather seeds together and in North Africa they have been observed to accumulate large piles of *Acacia* seeds. Any seeds collected from rodent or insect caches should be tested for soundness by cutting test or other means.

Collection from the Crowns of Felled Trees

One method of collecting large amounts of seed is to synchronise it with normal commercial fellings carried out during the seed ripening season and to collect seeds or fruits from felled trees. If fruits are to be collected from throughout the felled crop, picking should for safety reasons be postponed until felling in the area is complete. If phenotypic quality of parent trees is more important than quantity of seed, it is preferable to select, mark and, if possible, fell and harvest fruits from superior mother trees in advance of the main felling. In *Pinus radiata* plantations due for clear-felling in New Zealand, a method has been used whereby a trained forest officer selected and marked the best 8-13 stems per hectare and the seed collection gang felled and trimmed the trees and collected the cones, so as to leave no obstructions for the subsequent felling of the remaining trees. Collection of fruits from early thinnings should be avoided, since it is difficult to judge phenotypic quality correctly at that age. Felling crowns into existing gaps is advisable in order to facilitate recovery of cones. It is essential to confine collection to the season when seeds are mature; adjustment of felling dates to coincide with seed ripeness should be possible wherever the same authority is responsible for both the felling and the collecting activities, e.g. national forest services operating within state forests. Hand picking of cones or fruits in the fallen crowns is common practice, assisted by rakes, hooks or machetes. Small cluster-type cones, such as those of *Thuja* and *Tsuga*, may be harvested by cutting off the cone-laden branch tips and pulling them through a cone stripper. The stripper contains a series of teeth, similar to a rake, which are set sufficiently close together to remove the cones.

In practice collection in clear-felled areas has proved little if any cheaper than collecting from standing trees by a well-trained team of climbers, at least in north-temperate conifers. The tangle of fallen stems and crowns and the dispersal of some cones during felling greatly reduce productivity. Where operations are speedy and closely controlled, collection after the boles have been trimmed and removed but before the lop and top has been piled and burnt may prove the most efficient method.

Felling of selected individual trees specifically for seed collection may be necessary in areas where commercial fellings are not practised, for example when relatively small quantities of seed from a few trees are needed for provenance testing or other research purposes. Such special fellings should be avoided whenever possible, both because the bole is wasted and because the tree is lost as a future seed source, but they are sometimes inescapable in the case of tropical high forest species which are very difficult to climb and if a seed collecting expedition is severely limited in time. Felling tall but unbuttressed trees is usually a lot quicker than climbing them.

The collection of fruits from wind-thrown trees is generally undesirable, as little selection can be applied and there may be a bias towards trees with characteristics which pre-dispose them to wind damage.

Collection from Standing Trees with Access from the Ground

By hand

In the case of shrubs or low-branched trees, fruits can be picked directly from the branches by the collector while standing on the ground. Examples are *Crataegus*, *Sorbus* and *Ilex* spp. in temperate zones, the smaller acacias and mallee eucalypts in Australia and many of the small drought-resistant species of the arid and semi-arid zones. Smaller fruits are generally harvested directly into a basket, bag, bucket or other container held or worn by the picker.

Cutting, Breaking and Sawing

For branches out of arm's reach a variety of long-handled tools is available to enable the collector to reach the fruits from the ground. A pole and hook may be used to pull branches down within reach. Long-handled rakes, saws, chisels, hooks or pruning shears are used to pull off or sever individual fruits or fruit-bearing branchlets. Light rigid bamboo, aluminium or plastic poles 4-6 m in length are common. In order to reach beyond the 6-8 m range of single poles, multistage telescopic poles with a shear on the end have been developed. Researchers have noted that, in some species, fruits or cones on the lowest branches may yield little seed, because of lack of pollination in that position, and that it is therefore preferable to collect fruits from at least half way up the crown. Ability to use long-handled tools efficiently from the ground is much affected by the density and form of the crown in individual trees.

A rope can be thrown or pulled over a branch as already described, but used to break off the seed-bearing branch rather than to shake it. A thicker rope is needed than for shaking. The method is not recommended for general use. It damages the tree, allows access to pests and diseases and, in the case of pines and other species which take two years to mature their seeds, destroys the next year's seed crop while collecting the current year's.

Several types of *flexible saw* have been used successfully to sever branches from the ground. One model, described by Anon. 1979, consists of a 3 ft. long flexible cutting cable fitted with precision-set carbon steel teeth and two 35 ft. polypropylene control lines. A sand-filled safety weight is used to project one of the control lines over the branch. An earlier model, the "commando saw", now no longer in production, was effective in servering eucalypt branches in Australia. Two operators could bring down branches up to 20 cm in diameter quickly and easily.

The method is not applicable to trees with acutely angled branches such as *E. tereticornis*. The other limitation depends on the efficiency of projecting the line over the desired branch.

Rigid saws can also be used to sever branches. Researchers describe a method used in New Zealand in which a pruning saw or bow saw is attached by lugs to a 180 kg line running through a pulley previously raised into the crown. The pruning saw is used for small branches <2 cm diameter, while the bow saw will cut through a 10 cm branch in 5 minutes' sawing.

Use of Rifle

Another method of severing seed bearing branches is to shoot them down with a large calibre rifle. The method was successfully used to shoot out the tops of *Picea glauca* trees in seed production areas in north eastern USA. Not only was the topping of the trees found to be less expensive than climbing but the cones could also be collected at the best stage of development because of the short time in which the operation could be completed. More recently shooting off branches or tops from a helicopter has yielded promising results in Canada.

In Australia the collection of small samples of eucalypt and *Araucaria* seed from tall trees has been accomplished efficiently using a .222 or .243 or .308 calibre rifle with ×4 telescopic sights. Branches up to 15 cm diametre could be brought down. "Pointed soft point" ammunition is more effective than "hollow point" when used with a .308 rifle.

A disadvantage of the rifle method is that very strict safety precautions must be observed. There are limitations to where a rifle may be used, for example not near roads or built-up areas. Also crowns of some species such as *Araucaria* and *Picea* may be considerably damaged by this technique.

In shooting down branches it is usually necessary to steady the rifle on a tripod or to rest the stock against a tree or the side of a vehicle. A clear line of sight is required and this can be a limiting factor in dense forests. It is usually best to shoot at right angles to the branch and to sever the bark on the underside with the first shot to avoid branch hang-ups. The bark on the upper side is then cut and finally shots are placed at intervals across the branch. It is important to select branches which will fall unobstructed to the ground. Horizontal branches are more readily detached than ascending branches. The shots should be positioned to take advantage of branch leverage. The method is best suited for collecting research quantities of seed from a heavy seed crop clustered on branches or tops too inaccessible to be conveniently reached by other means.

Collection from Standing Trees with Access by Climbing

There is a limit to the height to which long-handled tools can be used for collecting seeds or fruits from the ground. Near that limit the operation consumes much time and energy but produces little seed. For tall trees which cannot be felled, therefore, climbing is often the only practical method of collecting. Some men are excellent natural climbers, while good training and good equipment can render collection by climbing an efficient and safe, albeit energetic, operation. For convenience the operation may be described under the following subheads:

(a) Climbing into the crown by way of the bole
(b) Climbing into the crown directly
(c) Climbing and picking of fruits within the crown.

Climbing into the Crown by Way of the Bole

Climbing with minimum equipment: Climbing without mechanical aids is practised in a number of countries. In the Philippines some seed collectors climb barefooted or with the help of a rope which ties both feet together and presses them against the trunk of the tree. Other modifications are for the climber to cut successive notches in the bole with a hand-axe to support his feet, or to hammer in a series of iron spikes about 20 cm long which are later withdrawn for re-use as he descends. Both of these methods are physically exhausting, whether or not a safety belt is used, and do some damage to the tree. Climbing tall branchless boles with hands and feet involves a considerable safety hazard and the risks may tempt climbers to prefer collecting from the most easily climbable trees which are often silviculturally the least desirable. It is preferable to introduce one or other of the special climbing aids now available.

Climbing irons or spurs, which are attached to the climber's boots, offer a light and inexpensive means of safer and more efficient climbing, if combined with safety belt, strap and line, safety helmet of glass fiber and heavy leather gloves. The lightness of the spurs (less than 1 kg a set) makes them particularly suitable for use in inaccessible stands in roadless country, where all equipment must be carried on foot. They have been found to be the most efficient method for climbing trees of *Pinus kesiya* and *P. merkusii* in Thailand and for *P. caribaea* and *P. oocarpa* in Honduras and are in common use in many countries, especially for conifers.

There are a number of different types of climbing irons but basically they consist of a forged iron arm and connecting piece which terminates in a pointed spur. The iron must be fastened securely by a leather strap to the foot gear and sometimes to the leg of the climber. The spur may be of varying length but it is an advantage if the point does not extend beyond the sole of the boot, so that the climber can walk on the ground without difficulty. The optimum length of spur depends on the type of bark. 5 cm spurs are suitable for barkless telephone poles and thin-barked trees and are recommended for most species in Canada, while 9 cm spurs are better suited to species with soft, thick bark. Climbing irons should not be used when the bark is frozen and are not particularly safe on scaly bark.

Detailed guidance to the fitting, use and maintenance of treeclimbing spurs in Canada. The following description of climbing with spurs closely follows their account. The climber ascends the tree using a safety belt, with a safety strap or safety chain passed around the stem and hooked to the belt. A safety line is tied to the belt and two or more carabiners are clipped onto one of the belt rings. When climbing the stem, the climber must ensure that the spikes are well into the wood of the tree by keeping the knees out from the stem when setting the spur. The lower leg and ankle must be kept at a fair angle to the stem to prevent slipping and gouging the bark. The weight is kept on the feet spaced 15- 20 cm apart and the centre of gravity away from the stem. The hands and arms are used to balance by holding the safety strap firmly in both hands, rythmically pulling the body towards the tree, moving the strap as the weight on it is lifted and tightening it in the new position as the body moves back. The pull on the safety strap is from the arms in ascending and it should not be transferred to the safety belt except when the climber is in a resting position. When the safety strap is tight, each foot is moved in turn and the weight transferred to the other foot. The safety strap is never unclipped except to bypass branches too heavy to break off. A second safety strap or carabiner with safety rope should be fastened above the obstructive branch before the first strap is unclipped. When sound branches are reached, preferably at the bottom of the live crown, the safety line is passed through a carabiner fastened by rope above the first branch, the safety strap is unclipped, and the climber works his way into the live branches.

The main disadvantage of spurs is the damage they do to the bark, particularly of thin-barked species. If climbing is only occasional, this should not be excessive, but frequent climbing of the same tree, e.g. for pollination and seed collection in seed orchards, is liable to cause an unacceptable degree of damage; other climbing methods should then be preferred.

Ladders

For heights from about 8 to 40 metres, vertical scaling ladders in several sections provide a safe and convenient means of climbing the bole to the live crown. They can be made of a variety of materials including wood, aluminium, magnesium alloy etc., but each section must be light enough to be easily pulled up by the climber. The legs of the bottom section can be placed on adjustable platforms for greater stability. The length of each section varies between 1.8 and 3 m and its weight should not exceed 3-4 kg.

The bottom one or two sections of the ladder are set up parallel to the tree stem with the bracket at the top against the trunk. The climber ascends with his safety strap around both the trunk and the ladder until his shoulders are level with the top of the ladder and then fastens it to the trunk by a rope or chain. Subsequent sections are pulled up by rope and fitted into the section below. Each section is climbed and fastened to the tree in turn. The same procedure is used for climbing from bole into crown as described above for climbing irons. With the lighter sectional ladders the climber can carry two sections, each 2 m long, attached to his safety belt. If the bottom two sections of 3 m each are fitted together and raised into position from the ground, this means he can erect a total of 10 m before needing to use the tool line to haul up additional sections.

Sectional ladders may be designed as "one-legged" or "two-legged". Two-legged are more common. The "one-legged" ladder comprises a central support with small bars fixed as rungs alternately on either side and is attached by chain or rope to the tree. The central support is usually made of steel or wood, so these ladders are not very different in weight from "two-legged" types. They have the advantage of being easier to lodge on uneven ground and they are also more easily manoeuvred between the branches and on very sinuous stems.

Sectional ladders can be used without any risk of damage to the tree. They can be awkward to handle in stands with dense canopy or undergrowth and are much heavier to carry than climbing irons, especially if long clear boles impose the need for many ladder sections. They are also more expensive. They are therefore of limited use in inaccessible roadless country, but are ideal in seed orchards or plantations in flat topography.

The Swiss tree bicycle or "Baumvelo" is a device for climbing tall straight trees which are branch-free to the live crown. It is lighter to transport than sectional ladders but heavier than climbing irons. It does no damage to the tree. It is suitable for use on stems with diameters ranging from 30-80 cm. Researcher found it very useful for climbing pine trees in Mexico. In the UK it was found particularly useful for conifer species with large cones e.g. *Pinus*, *Picea*, *Pseudotsuga*, in which the collector seeds to move from branch to branch to pull off the cones, rather than remaining for long in the same part. Its use in that country is now, however, restricted mainly to research collections, since the increased area of mature plantations allows bulk seed collections to be made easily from felled trees and ladders are more convenient for seed orchard collections.

The tree bicycle contains two separate units, one for each foot. Each unit consists of an arm (longer in the upper, shorter in the lower unit) to which is fixed a rubber supporting block which rests against the trunk. The lower end of the arm carries a stirrup or pedal with strap and quick release clips, which holds the climber's foot. The upper end is attached to a steel band forming a circle of adjustable diameter around the stem. The tree bicycle is used in conjunction with safety harness or belt, support chain or strap, safety line, safety clips or carabiners and nylon ropes.

The climber continues to ascend until the upper steel band meets the lower living branches of the crown. He then reaches into the crown to fit a nylon safety rope to hold the safety line and proceeds to "park" the tree bicycle. The essential operation is to tighten the lower band of the bicycle so that it grips the stem tightly even when there is no weight on it; there is then no risk of the bicycle slipping down the stem out of the climber's reach. The climber opens the ankle clips on both stirrups, frees his feet from the straps, unhooks his safety strap and climbs into the crown.

The tree bicycle provides an extremely safe means of climbing straight branchless trees without damaging them and is lighter and more portable than sectional ladders. Some practice is needed but most men become competent and quick in its use within a few days. Its main disadvantages are the cost, the fact that its use is limited to a certain range of diameters and that, unlike ladders and climbing irons, it requires the bole to be pruned of branches all round the circumference up to the living crown. Where regular climbing of the same trees is foreseen, however, as in seed stands or seed orchards, the cost of thorough initial pruning is fully justified. It is advisable to work always with two tree-bicycles within call of each other, because a man in difficulties on a tree at a height greater than can be reached by a ladder can only be reached on another tree-bicycle, or by climbing irons.

Collection from Standing Trees with Other Means of Access

Some types of equipment have been designed to raise the collector mechanically to a level where he can reach the fruit-bearing portion of the crown, without having to climb at all. Limited trials have shown that cable systems supporting a carriage can move pickers alongside tree crowns. Although access to several trees is obtained with one setting, the installation is time consuming. The system would prove most profitable in a stand where repeated collections are to be made. Experiments have also been made with cables or platforms suspended from balloons or helicopters. Balloons are not considered practical, but helicopters may have a part to play in certain conditions. Probably the most practical of all mechanical devices to raise or lower a man to within reach of the fruit crop is the Extension Platform.

The extension platform of a type used for the installation of overhead electric cables has been used for seed collection in many countries. There are a number of models available, including ones with telescopic raising gear and hydraulically operated articulated steel booms built on a turn-table.

Researcher describes the AGP-12 articulated extension device which has been constructed in the USSR and researcher illustrate and explain the use of the British developed Simon hydraulic platform. The Russian machine could be used to collect seeds from trees to a height of 15 m and the Simon hydraulic platform to a height of 10-16 metres. They provide adequate working space for two men, who can dispense with safety-belts and associated gear. It was intended to develop a larger version of the Russian machine to reach to 30 m.

A trailer-mounted platform attached to, and powered by, an agricultural tractor has been developed in Australia for seed collections from heights up to 10 metres above the ground. This tractor-trailer unit is capable of being used almost anywhere a tractor can be safely worked. It is versatile and relatively low cost equipment. The Afron Hydraulic Drive Power Ladder has a lower reach (maximum picking height 7 m), but is highly manoeuvrable and is operated by a single person, since all the controls are on the picking platform. It is widely used in fruit orchards and could be a useful machine in intensively managed forest seed orchards provided that the trees are of moderate size. The hydraulic platforms are of most value when time and labour are short and fruits can be collected from accessible trees with good crops. Disadvantages of this equipment are the necessity for good access and the high capital cost. Where cone crops have been less accessible and prolific, the per unit cost of collection using the Simon hydraulic platform in the UK was found to be greater than using ladders or tree bicycles".

Productivity in Fruit Collection

There is little detailed information on productivity in fruit collection, especially for tropical species. Amounts collected per picker-day depend on a variety of factors which include not only the skill and energy of the picker but the size of fruits, the heaviness of the crop, the firmness of attachment of the peduncles, the presence of old or immature fruits on the branches which may confuse or slow down the pickers, the method of collection (by climbing, from felled trees, from the ground etc.) and miscellaneous factors such as weather, insects and travelling time. For *Pseudotsuga* in USA and Canada, Researchers quote the same average figure of 2-3 hectolitres of cones per picker-day, collected from about four trees by climbing. Researchers indicated that the same rate of production can be expected from felled *Pseudotsuga* trees as by climbing the standing trees. 4-5 hectolitres of cones per climber per day can be expected for *Pinus ponderosa* and around 0.5 hectolitre for smaller-coned species such as *Larix*, *Thuja* and *Tsuga*. In IUFRO collections made in *Pseudotsuga*, *Picea sitchensis* and *Abies grandis* in western North America, a team of 4 experienced climbers could complete one selected stand in a day, collecting from about 20 well spaced trees. In Thailand in stands of *Pinus kesiya* of medium size trees an average of 25-30 kg of cones is expected per climber-day, collected from 6 trees. In Honduras the collecting rate for *P. oocarpa* and *P. caribaea* averages 1 to 2.5 hectolitres from 3-5 trees per man-day, for a general bulk collection in an average crop. Researchers reported that an average collecting rate in European pine stands, 25 m tall and bearing average to good crops, with the use of climbing irons, was 20-50 kg of cones from 8-10 trees in a day, yielding 0.4 to 1.0 kg of seeds.

Training and Safety

Seed collection, especially by climbing, is arduous work and it is essential that climbers are carefully selected and well trained before they commence collecting operations. They need to be physically and mentally fit, with a natural aptitude for climbing and a combination of self-confidence and common sense. Any sizable collection programme should have a nucleus of at least one skilled climber on the permanent staff, who may be employed on other duties outside the seeding season. It will be his responsibility to conduct short training courses for any temporary climbers before the start of each collection season. Good pictorial illustrations are an invaluable training aid, especially where climbers are illiterate.

Safety precautions will vary according to local conditions and particularly the species of tree and the equipment and methods of collection used:

1. All equipment should be carefully stowed, both during transport in the field and while in store between collecting seasons.
2. Clothing should be strong, well fitting, and suited to the weather expected.
3. All equipment should be checked before it is used and, if there is doubt about its condition, it must not be used until repaired or replaced.

4. Do not climb in wet or very windy weather, nor in poor light as at dusk, nor when overtired.
5. Do not climb trees with obvious signs of stem rot, severe cankers or galls, split stems, double leaders, or other abnormalities indicative of mechanical weakness.
6. The safety line should be coiled on the ground before the climber ascends to avoid tangling or snagging the rope in the underbrush.
7. The anchorman should hold the safety line under one arm and over the other shoulder. It is wise to make a half turn around a neighbouring tree. This gives control and prevents the safety line from being pulled from his hands. Pull in and pay out the safety line by alternate hand grips. A sliding rope is difficult to control and can cause painful friction burns.
8. Never climb with anything tied or looped around the neck.
9. Safety helmets and goggles should be worn to prevent injury to the head and eyes in climbing rough, densely branched trees.
10. Stand on and grip branches close to the point of attachment to the main stem.
11. Watch for brittle branches; test doubtful branches before putting weight on them. Avoid branches with bark peeling from them - they are slippery. As far as possible, decide on the climbing route while still on the ground, especially for the branchy crown region.
12. The climber should have three points of support at all times (one hand and two feet or two hands and one foot), moving one limb at a time, except when attached to the tree by a safety strap or rope or when suspended on a safety line. Climb calmly with regular movements, taking short steps.
13. Do not carry tools while climbing the crown. If there is need for a pole pruner or cone rake etc., use a light tool

line to hoist the equipment to the working level. Leave the tool line attached to large tools as a lanyard while working. Return tools to the ground on the line, do not drop them or throw them down.

14. Beware of sharp branch stubs: they can snag clothing and may cause painful cuts and bruises.
15. Climb spirally or in a zigzag manner, or fasten safety strops to the stem so that you cannot fall more than 2 m before your weight comes onto the safety line.
16. The diameter of the main stem should not be less than 8 cm at waist level during climbing. If in doubt concerning security, do not hesitate to tie a safety strop to the stem at a safe level before climbing within reach of the seed-bearing crown.
17. While attaching safety rope, keep one arm securely around tree until the rope is fastened to safety belt.
18. Before letting go of the tree with your hands, test your weight against the safety rope and footholds.
19. When picking near the top of a tree, keep your body close to the stem, so that your weight bears down, not outward.
20. The safety strap should always be attached around the tree stem except while you are climbing or changing position in the crown or are suspended on the safety line.
21. Before dropping bags of cones or other material, be sure that the personnel on the ground are notified and are well clear.
22. When collecting fruits from a ladder, make fast the top of the ladder to the tree with a nylon strop. The ladder must be further steadied with two guylines.
23. Have a well-stocked first aid kit handy at the climbing site at all times.

8

Seed Selection

From a population genetics point of view, in the seed selection process farmers exercise selection pressure in an attempt to enhance favoured traits in their maize and lessen the influence of undesired ones. This ensures that certain traits are passed on to the next generation at a higher frequency. Furthermore, these traits are what define a variety in the eyes of farmers, and studies have argued that this selection process plays an important part in what structures diversity in farmers' fields. As demonstrated by researchers the dynamics of maize genetic diversity in the study area is a combination of geneflow and selection; without farmers' seed selection, maize populations in this region would not show the great morphological diversity observed.

Farmers' maize seed selection can take place at any time between harvest and the next planting. The period of time in which seed selection takes place can vary greatly; in some households it is an intense, focused activity of relatively short duration. However, in many households it is an activity that takes place little by little over a long period of time, that is, for several months.

Finally, some farmers organize their seed selection in a more step-wise fashion, whichcan take place over different periods of time, according to the convenience and traditions of the individual farm household. Both men and women participate in the different steps of the seed selection process, although, in some cases, depending on the household, it is regarded as the responsibility of someone in particular.

In the baseline study an attempt was made at quantifying the use of different seed selection practices and the results of this . Farmers' use of plant characteristics in relation to seed selection has been reported from other traditional agricultural systems, for example sorghum and pearl millet in Africa.

It is noticeable that only some 3 per cent do any preharvest selection, which means that most are only selecting on the traits of the ear and kernels, but not, for example, on the characteristics of the plant (or the length of the cropping season). This appears to be the common practice for farmer maize seed selection in Mexico.

These traits may, however, have been included when the seed was acquired in the first place. The baseline study investigated the use of four post-harvest selection practices:

1. The separation of the harvest in piles designated for seed or grain.
2. The selection of ears for seed and the subsequent shelling.
3. Selection of seed in connection with using the maize for consumption.
4. Selection of seed just before planting.

The post-harvest selection can be undertaken in different ways. However, a general feature that all have in common, is that selection is done as a twostage process, first selecting the ear, and then selecting the seed kernels within the ear.

One way is to separate the harvested ears into two groups: one for seed and another for grain. The farmers may store the seed as ears with the husk intact until shortly before planting; or, alternatively proceed to dehusk and shell it and store the seed as kernels. Rather than carry out the seed selection as a separate process it may also be done little bylittle, as the harvest is being used. In this case, as the family members use of the stored maize, they will separate out the best ears for seed selection. Finally, the actual selection of the individual kernels to be used as seed may be done just before the planting.

Valdeflores, the predominant combination is to separate the harvested ears into two groups and then shell them before storage. This is complemented by selection as the maize is being used. In Santa Ana Zegache the predominant selection method indicated is during use, and in San Pablo Huitzo the main method is the separation of ears into two groups. Finally, in Santo Tomás Mazaltepec and San Lorenzo Albarradas farmers often select seed when usingthe harvest. However, this is combined with other methods, and no single method or combination of methods is predominant. It should be noted that the processes of post-harvest seed selection and management often take place during a time span of several weeks or even months, and despite several efforts at categorizing or systematizing, in many cases it is not a neatly ordered process that can easily be divided into separate phases.

Selecting the Ears

In local seed management, seed selection depends on the individual farmer's perception of what are desirable traits, and what makes good seed. These criteria are socially constructed, based on local knowledge and passed on between people. It is information, which over time, has been challenged, discussed and maybe modified according to the experience of the individual farmers. Like any other form of technological knowledge, it is a product ofsocial processes in the community. Some households store their maize as ears, leaving the husk on for protection.

Others remove the husk and yet others both de-husk and shell the maize. Initially, all the harvested ears are usually piled up in a certain part of the household or patio, often separated by maize type, if the household in question grows several kinds of maize. A common practice is to undertake a first sorting that separates damaged or badly developed ears from the healthy and well-developed ones. If squash was planted together with the maize and harvested at the same time, it is now put in a separate pile.

The next step is de-husking. On every single ear, the husk is forced open, pulled free and removed from the ear. This is done by hand, leaving the maize ear bare. The quality of the ear is now readily assessed, and in general the farmers who dehusk the maize before storage also use this moment to separate out any badly developed or damaged ears, which in most cases are then set aside to be used for animal feed. Often the farmer also uses this moment to separate particularly 'good' seed ears, for example, for subsequent shelling and storage. In many cases farmers have a clear idea of what the 'ideal' ear of their particular maize looks like, and when selecting seed ears they often try to get as close to this 'ideotype' as possible. Similar practices and criteria have been reported.

As mentioned above, seed selection is carried out almost exclusively at postharvest and as a result the selection criteria are related almost entirely to the ear and kernel characteristics. The baseline study investigated the different selection criteria applied by the farmers in the region.The vast majority of farmers select for large cleanears with all grains filled. They also look for large clean kernels and grain uniformity.

Researchers are also concerned with ear weight, but less so in San Agustín Amatengo, Santo Tomás Mazaltepec and Valdeflores. Cob size is also a concern for just over half of the farmers. Husk cover, which is important both to prevent infestation by pests as well as being an ingredient for example for cooking tamales is of much less concern to farmers. A possible explanation is that themaize types cultivated in the study area generally all have good husk cover, and as such is not an issue in seed selection.

The selection of seed from the individual maize ears also has many similarities across households, although, at the same time the details or sequences may vary quite considerably from one farmer to another. Who is in charge of seed selection also varies from one household to another.

Similar to the selection of ears from which to take seed, many farmers favour large, clean and healthy looking kernels that live up to the individual farmer's idea of what characterizes his/her particular maize, for example, shape, size and colour of kernels. Another common criterion is that kernels that are selected for seed should have intact and spotless pedicels, as damaged or dark pedicels is interpreted as a sign of poor seed quality or doubtful germination ability. As researcher explained: As long as it hasits little heart, the white part in the middle, it has to germinate. Look, like this little maize grain, this little heart, and this is where the little maize plant will start. Likewise another woman commented that one must make sure that the seed has been specially selected, is clean and undamaged by insects.

That one will germinate Many farmers follow a practice of only selecting kernels from a particular part of the ear, for example, only the lower 1/2 2/3 of the ear or only the middle part of the ear. When asked about this practice, farmers normally explain that these kernels make the best seed. Farmers in the study area are often influenced by a logic of 'like produces like'. For example the maize plants take after the seed it germinates from: if you select only big and beautiful kernels for seed, this is how the maize will be. However, if you use seed that is *guioxito* (small), the maize that will grow from it will be equally *guioxito.*

The kernels at the top of the ear (and often also those at the bottom) are slightly asymmetrical and smallerthan the rest, and in general, farmers in the study area appear to believe that these kernels make a poorer seed and produce inferior plants. A similar thing takes place in relation to the selection of ears for seed selection; farmers choose beautiful, well-developed ears in order for next season's harvest to be one of beautiful, well-developed maize ears. On the other hand, farmers also sometimes experience difficulty in explaining the rationale behind their practice of choice. In that case many simply explain that this is what they were taught about selecting good maize seed, and this is how they have always done it.

Furthermore, the practice of taking seed only from certain parts of the ears appears to be a common practice, not only in Mexico, but also in other parts of the Americas, as well as elsewhere outside the centres of origin of maize. The basis of these practices are not entirely understood.

However the kernels from the ear tip are usually smaller, have poor reserves, and are often damaged by birds, insects, and fungi, which may justify their exclusion. The authors also mention that unpublished results from their own germination tests indicate that the kernels from the upper part of the maize ear demonstrate a slower and a lower germination rate than the kernels of the centre and the base of the ear. With regard to the kernels at the base of the ear, no clear justification for leaving these out from the seed selection exists from a scientific perspective.

As the first silks to appear emerge from the base of the ear, these kernels may be subject to a greater probability of self-pollination and therefore inbreeding, than other kernels.

Seed selection is another area in which maize stands out in comparison to other crops, such as beans or chickpeas. It is common practice among farmers in the study communities to save seed of various crops. However, whereas maize seed is specially selected and generally carefully stored separate from the rest of the maize, thereby constituting an altogether different category from maize grain, a similar practice does not seem to apply for beans or chickpeas.

Researcher explains: "Seed maize is bigger. The little maize kernels, the second class maize, are for eating, but in beans they are the same, there is only one class. Beans (seed) are mixed, they are not selected, you throw (sow) it even if it is small. In comparison, neither beans (seed) nor chickpea (seed), are selected '*revuelto*' (mixed) adding that if you want to plant chickpeas, you just get it from anywhere.

Harvest and Seed Storage

Storage temperature and seed moisture content are very important for maintaining maize seed quality in terms of germination rate and vigour. In many developing countries, farmers' own seed storage facilities may not be able to control temperatures and moisture levels effectively. As a result seed quality may deteriorate significantly after only one year or less.

Under average local storage conditions in the study area, maize seed can be stored for one to two years and still retain an acceptable germination rate andvigour, provided the maize seed is not damaged otherwise by storage pests, pathogens or fungi. Nevertheless, knowing that seed quality declines with prolonged storage, farmers clearly prefer to use seed that is as 'fresh' as possible.

Most farmers do not store maize seed longer than one or a maximum two seasons and poor germination rate is seldom a problem in relation to the seed the farmer selected him-/herself. However, seed quality remains a point of concern, especially in connection with seed acquisitions from other, unknown sources.

The harvest can be stored either as ears with or without husks, or shelled as kernels. San Pablo Huitzo, Santo Tomás Mazaltepec, San Lorenzo Albarradas, and Valdeflores, the preferred form of storage is as ears, whereas in San Agustín Amatengo and Santa Ana Zegache farmers predominantly store the harvest as kernels. For the latter it is somewhat surprising that on the question of seedselection they also indicated that this was done when using the grain. This must mean that the respondents understand 'use' as including the shelling of the ears before storage.

Farmers in the study area apply a variety of pesticides to protect the maize seed during storage, containing various kinds and concentrations of toxic substances. These include phostoxin, folidol and occasionally, lindane. Of these, the most widely used are the phostoxin tablets, and when used correctly this is also the least harmful to human health. The tablets react with air, dissolving slowly as a gas. The tablets are left among the maize to be stored; however, for the product to be effective, an airtight container must be used in order to contain the gas. Not all farmers who use this product are aware of the way it works. Many store their grain or seed in ordinary sacks or large finely woven baskets; however, as these are not airtight, the effect of the tablets is significantly reduced unless lined with plastic. At the same time, it is quite common that farmers exceed the recommended dosage per volume of maize – sometimes deliberately in order to counter what appears to be a weak effect of the tablets. Nevertheless, some farmers are concerned about the poisonous effect and do not treat the maize intended for consumption.

When folidol or lindane is applied, it is usually in a powder version. If the farmer stores the seed as whole ears it is common to simply sprinkle the ears with the powder. If the seed is shelled the powder is added and mixed well with the maize.

Among artisanal methods, the most commonly mentioned is the application of lime, or in some cases, ashes, which is simply mixed with the shelled maize seed, and provides a certain level of protection against insects. Some farm households also use chilli or herbs to protect the seed against storage pests, for example, Felipa and Santos, mentioned in the section on seed acquisition.

Farmers use a variety of containers for seed storage, although plain nylon sacks are the most common. Some farmers recognize the disadvantages of just using plain sacks and devise their own solutions to grain/ seed storage. For example, Pablo Lopez (Huitzo) stores his maize seed in a tightly sealed barrel/ oil drum, and Doña Rosa (Zegache) uses nylon sacks, but lines them with heavy-duty plastic sacks in order to contain the effect of the tablets she applies against storage insects. Others use heavy-duty plastic buckets withtightly fitting lids, and for very small seed quantities I have also seen emptied soft-drink bottles with screw-lids used.

A smaller number of households in the study communities own a small-scale metal silo specifically designed for small-scale farmers' grain storage. During initial phase of the CIMMYT-INIFAP project farmers complained about the high rates of grain and seed losses in storage. As a response the CIMMYTINIFAP project staff provided training on a series of practices and technologies which could help improve storage conditions and diminish storage losses, including a simple type of metal silo that some farmers in San Agustín Amatengo were already using. The silos were tested in the other study communities and a rotating financial scheme was set up in order to help interested farmers acquire a silo of the preferred dimensions. The principle of the silos is to effectively prevent mice and rats from having access to the maize stored in it, while at the same time protecting the grain against insect infestation. The latter is achieved by making sure that the grain is not infested at the moment when the silo is filled, and subsequently by the lack of oxygen in the full silo.

Where farmers store the maize seed is yet another detail. The granary or *troje* is normally outside the house, but somewhere in the patio where household animals cannot easily get to it. Shelled grain is often stored on the porch, in an outhouse or in connection to the cooking shed/kitchen. However, the prepared (i.e. shelled and possibly treated) maize seed is often stored inside the house or, alternatively, somewhere else considered equally secure.

Some farmers will check the state of their maize seed once or twice during the storage period, cleaning it and removing any infested kernels and maybe re-applying treatment against storage pests.

The widespread practice of selecting seed based on ear and kernel criteria alone, means that traits, which maintenance depends on selection related to other parts of the plant, are left out of the selection process. Obviously, this would also exclude selecting for traits which cannot be seen with the human eye or otherwise easily observed, for example, the contents of lysine and tryptophan in the case of QPM-Maize. Other traits - length of production cycle, or other aspects of the plant - are taken into account at the time when the farmer decides what maize to plant. It is important to keep in mind that this decision, that is to say, varietal selection, has a considerably larger impact on production and consumption characteristics, than does seed selection from one cycle to the next.

On-farm seed management practices are based on performative knowledge, and the above description illustrates a range of issues in trying to verbalize this knowledge. Especially, when looking at the data from the surveys, these problems become obvious. For example, the ambiguity of the term 'in use' made it difficult to understand seed practices in Santa Ana. Almost all answered that they selected the ears for seed when using the maize ; however, they also store the maize as kernels meaning that they shell it before storage. The use therefore refers to the shelling rather than to the use for consumption. This also illustrates the problem of taking a complex activity, such as seed management where the farmers draw on a wide range of knowledge, and apply different options in a flexible manner according to the circumstances, and trying to break this down into a series of yes/no questions.

The seed selection process has been broken down into a numberof practices, and organized in a presumed systematic and chronological way, but this does not seem to appear particularly relevant to farmers and is not in accordance with their perception of seed practices. However, interviewees often tried to accommodate and answer within the options provided.

It should be emphasized here, that the Later in the research process, it became clear that many farmers in the study communities did not organize their seed management practices in a systematic sequence of clearly defined and separate steps. Rather, seed management is done in a parallel and multi-tasked fashion and forms an integral part of harvest management. Many of the initial steps are not seed management ac-29 compared to other types of maize, Quality

Protein Maize (QPM) contains nearly twice as much of two key amino acids - lysine and tryptophan – which make protein usable for humans and monograstric animals. Quality Protein Maize is considered able to improve the diets of people who consume mainly maize. Furthermore, used as feed, it is assumed that QPM can provide poor farmers with a means for improving livestock production, and thereby, for new income-earning strategies. QPM is grown on more than 0.5 million hectares in 22 developing countries.

It is currently not grown in the study area. Acivities as such, but simply harvest management, where seed selection may occur in an opportunistic manner, whenever one has a moment or comes across particularly good seed material. Seed selection as such is not carried out as one continuous activity where each step is completed in a relatively short, coherent time span. Several parts of the process may be initiated simultaneously and interrupted various times over a total period of several weeks or months. The interruptions are often not motivated by technical issues or seed management considerations, but are much more of a resource management issue, where work is undertaken when time between other tasks and events permits it.

The situation is similar with regards to seed storage practices. The tables presented here could be said to convey a 'deceptionally clear' picture of local seed storage practices. However, as with other harvest and seed management practices, the preparation and organisation of seed storage is often undertaken in parallel with, or according to how, other activities or events unfold, much along the lines of Richards' reflections on agriculture as a performance. The issues raised in this section illustrate the problems that were repeatedly mentioned in relation to efforts to 'translate' performative into verbalized knowledge and vice versa. The results of such efforts often include categories that appear unclear or ambiguous, and the loss of internal logic as complex processes are broken down into separate elements. In short, as pointed out earlier, efforts to 'translate' one kind of knowledge into another necessarily imply a transformation and often also simplification of the knowledge involved.

The aspects presented here also highlight some of the problems in trying to systematize local knowledge. In a review of the development of the study of local knowledge, explains that early efforts to recognize and incorporate local knowledge into the development debate tended to assume that it could be conceived of as a 'system', a fact which often led to the simplification of local knowledge. As Pottier notes, it has since become increasingly clear that knowledge changes and evolves continuously, not necessarily in a systematic way, nor is it necessarily organized. As a result the notion of 'knowledge systems' and their presumed boundedness is increasingly challenged.

Attempts to organize farmers' seed practices in terms of a seed system encounter difficulties both with regard to the need for defining the constituting elements of the system, such as seed, varieties, and management practices, as well as in relation to defining the boundaries of the system itself. In the findings above I have discussed how both seed, and especially varieties, are flexibleconcepts that cannot easily be 'fitted into' a clear definition related to an element of a system. Likewise, in presenting the seed management practices, it was clear that many different ways of doing similar tasks exist, and these may be combined in different ways.

The specific choice of practice is often influenced by factors such as availability of labour or the personal preferences of the farmer at a given moment. The seed management practices are also difficult to pin down. Seed selection, for example, has considerable flexibility in terms of when it is carried out, and this flexibility is used by the farmers to complete it as *ad hoc* parts of other practices over an extended period of time. This means that several activities, which in fact are integral parts of other practices, such as post-harvest management, contribute to the same end, for example seed selection. As such, these practices cannot easily be separated from other practices and this leads to difficulties in delimiting the seed system.

In short, several aspects of on-farm seed management practices, including seed selection, form part of general post-harvest management, or are carried out in relation to using the harvest for consumption. Thus isolating or separating seed selection is problematic. Furthermore, seed exchange practices are also embedded in more general social relations, and must be analysed in relation to this more general social network. As such, both on-farm and off-farm seed practices are difficult to isolate as individual, clearly delimited parts of a seed system.

It is possible to construct a system for just about anything and thus it is also possible to consider the Oaxacan farmers' seed practices as a system. However, doing this inevitably implies a gross simplification of local knowledge and a process of 'disambiguation' of farmers' seed concepts. It also leads to difficulties in delimiting the seed system in relation to other practices both onand off-farm.

The widely used term 'informal seed systems' or 'farmers' seedsystems' implies that these should be analysed as systems, but this research questions the very notion. Instead, it is proposed to focus on seed practices, and to ensure that the analysis takes the ambiguities in farmers' seed concepts, as well as the flexibility in their seed practices, into proper account.

Furthermore, it considers farmers' seed practices as integral parts of other onand off-farm practices. Performative knowledge is not only a question of technical and practical skill in relation to undertaking a given activity. As pointed out by researcher, the knowledge required often also includes moral dimensions such as,for example, how to promote one's own status, obligations and responsibilities towards others.

The notion of 'status' refers to one's position in society, particularly the position that other people attribute to one, that is, the prestige or importance that one acquires in the eyes of other people. Meanwhile the term 'reputation' refers to the opinion that other people have of someone as a result of what he/she does and how he/she behaves. The two are obviously closely related, yet, high status is not automatically linked to good reputation and vice versa.

Social roles are also closely related to status. However, one's status may change depending on the social context – in fact sociologists talk about 'sets of statuses' referring to the individual's various statuses in different social contexts. Often a distinction is made between ascribed status based on biological factors, for example, age, sex, race; and achieved status, which refers to the individual's efforts and achievements in his/her life course. While aspects such as structural positions and roles can be considered human accomplishments, they have real consequences for the people who occupy them.

Social interaction is always situated in time and space and may involve different forms of verbal and non-verbal communication. Everyday interaction depends on subtle relationships between what we convey with our faces and bodies and what we express in words. The ability to interpret and accord meaning to social situations, in order to draw on the role or positional knowledge acquired during socialization, is therefore an important interactional skill, given that improvisation and negotiation are essential features in the construction of social action. The study of how people make sense of what others do and say has been called ethnomethodology.

The metaphor of the theatre has also been used as a framework for the analysis of social interaction and everyday life, among others, who gives central attention to how social roles are constructed and performed. This notion also refers to the socially defined expectations of an individual in a given status or social position. Following the theatre metaphor, in the various contexts of social life there tend to be clear distinctions between 'on-stage' and 'off-stage' situations, where actors prepare themselvesfor the performance and relax afterward. A good example of this is Goffman's classic study of self representation in everyday life, where he demonstrates how social actors, playing out their roles, are sensitive about how they are seen by others, and hence try to manage the impressions they give. Impression management can take many forms, the most common probably being the unconscious following of norms, for example, dressing appropriately for a business meeting or for church.

Elsewhere in this chapter the notion of 'the good farmer' which refers, admittedly in a rather nebulous or fuzzy way, to an ideal embodying a series of aspects that are highly valued in others by the farmers in this region, and which includes issues such as personal integrity, independence and respect.

At the same time the idea of 'the good farmer' includes a series of common, local values regarding farming and being a fellow community member touched upon again in subsequent chapters in relation to trust, mutual help and reciprocity).

As a member of the community one is expected to take part in various community issues and *tequios* and contribute one's due share in relation to both actual financial contributions as well as in terms of public service or the responsibilities that one may be appointed to. After several years abroad as a migrant worker, Don Jesus returned to his community, when he was appointed for a public responsibility. Jesus explained that while he saw it both as an honour and an obligation, he also realized that refusing the chargewould eventually have made it very difficult for him to return to the community at a later stage and still be respected as a full community member.

Other community member obligations are easier to negotiate. For example, failure to participate in *tequios* and other community works is often sanctioned, for example by a 'fine' or, eventually, by loss of certain rights, which can then only be regained through compensation. People who know beforehand that they cannot participate, sometimes make arrangements to send someone else in their place, or, as is sometimes done in the case of migrants, monetary compensation is agreed upon with the authorities and sent from abroad or paid by family members in the community. As with other farming practices, certain aspects of seed management seem to influence one's standing and reputation as a 'good farmer'. For example, knowing how to select and manage maize seed appears to be regarded as a valuable and central skill.

People who do not produce their own seed are frowned upon; sometimes even regarded as lazy or not very good farmers. A discussion regarding this issue developed spontaneously during the men's focus group discussion in San Lorenzo Albarradas, during which the majority of the group quickly established that this applied to 'farmers, who don't know how to do their job properly, or who are lazy, do not select and save seedfrom the previous harvest' . Or note Liliana's comment, with a clearly reproachful tone to it: "Why do you ask for seed, if you have maize?!" Likewise, in relation to mutual helpfulness, people, who are known to have plenty of seed, but who are nevertheless not willing to provide seed to others, are thought of as selfish.

Living up to the role of the good farmer also implies not taking undue advantage of another farmer in need: one should be honest and not take advantage of a fellow farmer/villager (e.g. farmers). This is especially so if the person is in a difficult situation, such as lacking seed in the middle of the planting season. Rodolfo, for example, still held a grudge against the person who sold him seed, but used the occasion to press the price up, on one occasion where he still had land left to plant, but had already run out of seed.

This is consistent with data from the in-depth interviews, revealing what appears to be a strong cultural value in the study area associated with being helpful to others, as long as one is able to do so while covering one's own needs. Likewise, in connection to this, an important motivating factor for many seed providers is that the person requesting the seed has a genuine need for it. This was an aspect, which arose during almost all the focus group interviews. Finally, it should be mentioned that this also appears to be part of a common sense of reciprocity.

As mentioned earlier, the study of local knowledge should also include consideration of moral aspects or values. Similar to the point that Marchand makes, about the kind of moral knowledge required to be a master builder in Yemen being a 'good farmer' in the study area also contains moral components.

For example, there are aspects of 'the good farmer' which have more to do with social and cultural values than strictly with farming, for example, being helpful towards others, doing one's fair share of community work, taking part in reciprocity and exchange, and answering to social obligations in general.

With specific regard to farmers' maize seed practices, this is expressed in the custom of saving seed, as well as in relation to a common sense of social responsibility which includes being willing to supply seed to a fellow farmer in need, as far as one is able to, and one is generally pressed to do this and other favours in a way that does not take undue advantage of the other farmer's need.

Like much other performative knowledge related to seed practices, the issues of how to be a good farmer and community member, and gain others' respect clearly influence people's practices. This is often reflected in the strategic representation of local knowledge and in people's individual self-representation.

The way farmers present their local knowledge is influenced by the situation in which they find themselves and by whom they are communicating with and who else is present, but also by how the farmers would like to present themselves. Hence, farmers often do not only represent what they do, but also what they would like to be doing. For example, when describing particular practices or different aspects of community life, many had a tendency only todescribe the 'good' version, that is one which is, if not ideal then at least acceptable according to local codes of practice and interaction. Meanwhile, the 'bad' or less acceptable version is always about other people.

Methodologically these are not aspects that are prone to surface, for example, in the application of formal questionnaires. Rather, these and similar issues are better illuminated through the use of more qualitative approaches. The degree to which, in this research, farmers 'negotiated' their representation of local knowledge in a strategic way is difficult to estimate.

The long term interaction with CIMMYT researchers, at different intensities and intervals and through a wide variety of modalities, as well as thetransparent approach adopted by the institution with regard to research objectives and resources, no doubt served to establish a certain trust and credibility in the relationship between farmers and researchers. However, there is little doubt that some degree of negotiation did take place, both by farmers and by researchers, seeking to explore the possibilities of furthering one's chances of obtaining favours, information, prestige and so forth. Still, this does not necessarily affect research in a negative way - after all this is the usual way, in which knowledge processes and much communication between social actors take place.

9 Seed Dormancy

Seed dormancy is a condition of plant seeds that prevents germinating under optimal environmental conditions. Living, non dormant seeds germinate when soil temperatures and moisture conditions are suited for cellular processes and division; dormant seeds do not.

One important function of most seeds is delayed germination, which allows time for dispersal and prevents germination of all the seeds at same time. The staggering of germination safeguards some seeds and seedlings from suffering damage or death from short periods of bad weather or from transient herbivores; it also allows some seeds to germinate when competition from other plants for light and water might be less intense. Another form of delayed seed germination is seed quiescence, which is different than true seed dormancy and occurs when a seed fails to germinate because the external environmental conditions are too dry or warm or cold for germination. Many species of plants have seeds that delay germination for many months or years, and some seeds can remain in the soil seed bank for more than 50 years before germination. Some seeds have a very long viability period, and the oldest documented germinating seed was nearly 2000 years old based on radiocarbon dating .

True dormancy or innate dormancy is caused by conditions within the seed that prevent germination under normally ideal conditions. Often seed dormancy is divided into two major categories based on what part of the seed produces dormancy: exogenous and endogenous. There are three types of dormancy based on their mode of action: physical, physiological and morphological.

There have been a number of classification schemes developed to group different dormant seeds, but none have gained universal usage. Dormancy occurs because of a wide range of reasons that often overlap, producing conditions in which definitive categorisation is not clear. Compounding this problem is that the same seed that is dormant for one reason at a given point may be dormant because of another reason at a later point. Some seeds fluctuate from periods of dormancy to non dormancy, and despite the fact that a dormant seed appears to be static or inert, in reality they are still receiving and responding to environmental cues.

Exogenous Dormancy

Exogenous dormancy is caused by conditions outside the embryo and is often broken down into three subgroups:

Physical Dormancy

Which occurs when seeds are impermeable to water or the exchange of gases. Legumes are typical examples of physically dormant seeds; they have low moisture content and are prevented from imbibing water by the seed coat. Chipping or cracking of the seed coat or any other coverings allows water intake. Impermeability is often caused by an outer cell layer which is composed of macrosclereid cells or the outer layer is composed of a mucilaginous cell layer. The third cause of seed coat impermeability is a hardened endocarp. Seed coats that are impermeable to water and gases form during the last stages of seed development.

Mechanical Dormancy

Mechanical dormancy occurs when seed coats or other coverings are too hard to allow the embryo to expand during germination. In the past this mechanism of dormancy was ascribed to a number of species that have been found to have endogenous factors for their dormancy instead. These endogenous facts include physiologically dormancy cased by low embryo growth potential.

Chemical Dormancy

Includes growth regulators etc, that are present in the coverings around the embryo. They may be leached out of the tissues by washing or soaking the seed, or deactivated by other means. Other chemicals that prevent germination are washed out of the seeds by rainwater or snow melt.

Endogenous Dormancy

Endogenous dormancy is caused by conditions within the embryo itself, and it is also often broken down into three subgroups: physiological dormancy, morphological dormancy and combined dormancy, each of these groups may also have subgroups.

Physiological Dormancy

Physiological dormancy prevents embryo growth and seed germination until chemical changes occur. These chemicals include inhibitors that often retard embryo growth to the point where it is not strong enough to break through the seed coat or other tissues. Physiological dormancy is indicated when an increase in germination rate occurs after an application of gibberellic acid (GA3) or after Dry after-ripening or dry storage. It is also indicated when dormant seed embryos are excised and produce healthy seedlings: or when up to 3 months of cold (0-10°C) or warm (=15°C) stratification increases germination: or when dry after-ripening shortens the cold stratification period required. In some seeds physiological dormancy is indicated when scarification increases germination.

Physiological dormancy is broken when inhibiting chemicals are broken down or are no longer produced by the seed; often by a period of cool moist conditions, normally below (+4°C) 39°F, or in the case of many species in *Ranunculaceae* and a few others,(-5°C) 24°F. Abscisic acid is usually the growth inhibitor in seeds and its production can be affected by light. Some plants like *Peony* species have multiple types of physiological dormancy, one affects radicle (root) growth while the other affects plumule (shoot) growth. Seeds with physiological dormancy most often do not germinate even after the seed coat or other structures that interfere with embryo growth are removed. Conditions that affect physiological dormancy of seeds include:

- **Drying**; some plants including a number of grasses and those from seasonally arid regions need a period of drying before they will germinate, the seeds are released but need to have a lower moister content before germination can begin. If the seeds remain moist after dispersal, germination can be delayed for many months or even years. Many herbaceous plants from temperate climate zones have physiological dormancy that disappears with drying of the seeds. Other species will germinate after dispersal only under very narrow temperature ranges, but as the seeds dry they are able to germinate over a wider temperature range.
- **Photodormancy** or light sensitivity affects germination of some seeds. These photoblastic seeds need a period of darkness or light to germinate. In species with thin seed coats, light may be able to penetrate into the dormant embryo. The presence of light or the absence of light may trigger the germination process, inhibiting germination in some seeds buried too deeply or in others not buried in the soil.
- **Thermodormancy** is seed sensitivity to heat or cold. Some seeds including ocklebur and amaranth germinate only at high temperatures (30°C or 86°F) many plants that have seed that germinate in early to mid summer have thermodormancy and germinate only when the soil temperature is warm. Other seeds need cool soils to germinate, while others like celery are inhibited when soil temperatures are too warm. Often thermodormancy requirements disappear as the seed ages or dries.

Seeds are classified as having deep physiological dormancy under these conditions: applications of GA3 does not increase germination; or when excised embryos produce abnormal seedlings; or when seeds require more than three months of cold stratification to germinate.

Morphological Dormancy

Embryo underdeveloped or undifferentiated. Some seeds have fully differentiated embryos that need to grow more before seed germination, or the embryos are not differentiated into different tissues at the time of fruit ripening.

Immature embryos - some plants release their seeds before the tissues of the embryos have fully differentiated, and the seeds ripen after they take in water while on the ground, germination can be delayed from a few weeks to a few months.

Combined Dormancy

Seeds have both morphological and physiological dormancy.

Morpho-physiological or morphophysiological dormancy occurs when seeds with underdeveloped embryos, also have physiological components to dormancy. These seeds therefore require dormancy-breaking treatments as well as a period of time to develop fully grown embryos.

- Intermediate simple
- Deep simple
- Deep simple epicotyl
- Deep simple double
- Intermediate complex
- Deep complex

Combinational Dormancy

Combinational dormancy occurs in some seeds, where dormancy is caused by both exogenous (physical) and endogenous (physiological) conditions. some *Iris* species have both hard impermeable seeds coats and physiological dormancy.

Secondary Dormancy

Secondary dormancy occurs in some non-dormant and post dormant seeds that are exposed to conditions that are not favourable for germination, like high temperatures. It is caused by conditions that occur after the seed has been dispersed. The mechanisms of secondary dormancy are not yet fully understood but might involve the loss of sensitivity in receptors in the plasma membrane.

Not all seeds undergo a period of dormancy, many species of plants release their seeds late in the year when the soil temperature is too low for germination or when the environment is dry. If these seeds are collected and sown in an environment that is warm enough, and/or moist enough, they will germinate. Under natural conditions non dormant seeds released late in the growing season wait until spring when the soil temperature rises or in the case of seeds dispersed during dry periods until it rains and there is enough soil moisture.

Seeds that do not germinate because they have fleshy fruits that retard germination are quiescent, not dormant.

Many garden plants have seeds that will germinate readily as soon as they have water and are warm enough, though their wild ancestors had dormancy. These cultivated plants lack seed dormancy because of generations of selective pressure by plant breeders and gardeners that grew and kept plants that lacked dormancy.

Seeds of some mangroves are viviparous and begin to germinate while still attached to the parent; they produce a large, heavy root, which allows the seed to penetrate into the ground when it falls.

10 Informal Seed Exchange

Research in the Central Valleys indicated that farmers who needed to acquire seed from other farmers experienced some difficulty in finding seed that met their requirements. First, a farmer has to learn who grows which maize variety and investigate the characteristics and performance of the maize of interest. Then he or she must make sure that the information offered is trustworthy and the seed is reliable. Finally, the conditions of acquiring the seed must be negotiated.

It therefore appears that acquiring seed of diversemaize varieties under these conditions can entail risks and high transaction costs to individual farmers. If one assumes that there is a high probability of seed loss due to climatic conditions and poor storage, then it is reasonable to hypothesize that a group of farmers could maintain more diversity than any individual, at a lower cost and with reduced probability of loss.

There should be clear incentives for individual farmers to cooperate in providing seed and information for a diverse set of maize varieties—in other words, for engaging in collective action to support their seed supply. The basic ingredients for collective action are present: a group of farmers with a common interest and a benefit that accrues from a voluntary group action. Furthermore, in this region several traditional collective action institutions exist, such as the *tequio* To test this hypothesis, the following operational definition of collective actionwas developed, based on the notions of collective action reviewed earlier:

> The actions of a well-defined group of farmers linked by a set of rights and responsibilities regarding the mutual supply of seed of a diverse set of farmer varieties.

Building on this definition, the following predictions were developed in order to examine the hypothesis:

This is reasonable because rainfed agriculture predominates in the area, with common occurrence of severe drought. For example, during the period of the study 1997-2002 there were two years with major droughts. Furthermore, drought and storage losses were identified as very important concerns by these farmers. It refers to a form of comunal work in which one has to provide a service to the community.

It can refer to comunal work in the interest of a certain group (for example, the local school), or it can be in the interest of the community in general (for example,construction and maintenance of roads, drinking water, infrastructure, or sewerage). It is a Zapotec institution of mutual aid between households. It can take place in many different situations and between different people and includes agricultural tasks, the roofing of houses, weddings, funerals, and religious festivals.

The existence of a number of people that identify themselves as part of a group that recurrently shares seed in some form (e.g., sale, exchange, or barter).

- Apart from the existence of a group, collective action could be inferred from adherence to a certain set of rights and responsibilities regarding the mutual supply of seed. This behaviour should be reflected in how seed transactions are conducted (e.g., specific practices or patterns associated with seed flows).
- The existence of collective action should depend on providing certain advantages or benefits to farmers compared to working individually. These could include

lower transaction costs for acquiring seed or reduced risk of seed shortages. Saving seed from one's own harvest is the predominant practice in the study area. Previous research showed that 89.7 per cent of all seed lots were saved by farmers from their own previous harvest, and the rest were acquired from other farmers. Only 24.2 per cent and 20.9 per cent of the farmers in the tracer study acquired or distributed seed, respectively, in 2001. Farmers in the tracer study said that their main reasons for acquiring seed were for experimentation and, to a much lesser extent, to overcome the lack of seed of their own. The main reason for giving seed to others was a sense of social responsibility.

Farmers felt that they were morally obliged to give seed to the farmer who asked for it. Most transactions involved the exchange of money or seed, and some farmers said explicitly that they engaged in seed transactions to obtain seed or money, but often the reason to engage in the transaction was not the payment *per se.* Many types of seed transactions were identified.

Types of Seed Transactions

Informants described different types of seed transactions in detail during the ethnographic interviews and focus group discussions. Quantitative data on seed transactions were later gathered in the seed flow tracer study. Transactions were classified into seven categories, including 'other', which referred to infrequent, *ad hoc* transactions.

The quantitative data clearly show the heterogeneity of transactions, although purchases account for half of all transactions. Focus group discussions and informant interviews provided detail on the many types of transactions and their individual variations. The hypothesis predicted a relatively uniform and clearly defined mode of transaction, reflecting adherence to a set of rights and responsibilities and a system of collective action. This was not what was found. In addition, although most informants remembered from whom they had obtained seed in the recent past, many had difficulty recalling to whom they had given seed, which may explain the noticeable discrepancy between the number of acquisitions and distributions.

Most seed transactions carry no obligation beyond the immediate transaction, except for borrowed seed or seed given as a gift. The borrower must repay the seed, and gifts usually carry an implicit obligation to return the favour. Transactions involved different types of social relations between the seed.

Purchase is the form of transaction least dependent on the social relation between the two parties. In fact farmers in general say that this type of transaction can be done with any person. This is confirmed by the findings from previous CIMMYT studies in the region. The exception would be the farmers who will only distribute seed to other farmers if they are confident that this other person will observe the general norm of taking good care of the seed and be very careful not to lose it again. Of all the farmers interviewed for this study in particular, none had any reservations with regards to selling seed to others, provided they could spare the seed and were appropriately compensated. In Frida's household for example, they cannot spare much maize, whether grain or seed, and in general they do not sell. Only if another family member or a very close friend asks, but then just 2-3 kilos, no more says Frida.

The person who needs to acquire seed will approach a possible seed provider. Then he asks: 'Will you sell me a bit of maize seed?' One then says yes or no. If there is seed, then 'yes, only, you will have to pay so and so'. And if there is not, then one says 'I haven't got any [seed], but I have maize grain, but it is good, it is big, almost the same as the seed.' Then it's up to the other person .

It should be pointed out that in this region the price of local maize seed is about twice the price of grain, while the price of a commercial hybrid will be in the order of 8-10 times the price of grain.

Hybrid seed costs several times the price of local seed and can normally not be acquired in the communities. However, the price of the seed - whether land race, hybrid or other, is still minimal compared to other production costs. That is, though probably the most important input, the seed is also one of the cheapest. Nevertheless, farmers often state the price of hybrid seed as a reason for not using it. Furthermore, farmers normally emphasize that hybrid varieties need more water than local maize landraces and longer time to mature. Finally, but maybe most importantly, for their own consumption these farmers prefer local landraces. When hybrids are sown, it is mostly for animal fodder or, in smaller quantities, for *elotes*, i.e. corn-on-the-cob, a popular snack.

From the word c*ompadrazgo,* referring to a ritual kinship somewhat similar to the relation known elsewhere as godparents, through which close relations of loyalty, mutual help, reciprocity, and confidence are established and formalized. Often there is a certain degree of prestige associated with being asked to become someone's *compadre* or *comadre*, and in some ways *compadrazgo* can signify social capital. Informants stress the issue of trust as very important in this case.

That's where people's friendships come in – not just anybody is going to lend you something like that. It will be because they trust you are going to give it back. The reason is obvious: this type of transaction implies a risk for the seed provider that the receiver of the seed will forget, or not be able to fulfil his/her part of the deal, which is, to give back same quantity and quality of seed after the first harvest.

Exchanging Seed

Another type of transaction is exchange of seed. Josefina explains this transaction in the following way: If you bring one almud of white maize (seed), we will exchange it for one almud of black maize [seed] '*a cambio*' (in exchange). If one wants black, if one wants yellow, *belatove*...the colour one wants, you go and bring your maize (seed).

Exchange appears to be less problematic than lending. The 'handover' and 'payment' takes place at the same time, and the seed provider avoids the risk of not being paid. Nevertheless, judging from these and other interviews many seed providers still have some reservations about exchange. The issue seems to be the uncertainty about whether the provider receives seed of a satisfactory quality in return for his/her seed. While selling/purchase does not seem to present a problem for most seed providers, obtaining the money to pay for the seed can be a problem for somefarmers seeking seed.

They may have an advantage in exchange or lending instead of purchasing. However, unless the person asking for the seed is trusted, seed providers tend to prefer selling/ purchase as the type of transaction, as this helps them avoid the risks of lack of payment or of receiving low quality kernels in return for their own specially selected seed.

The in-depth interviews and focus group discussions revealed the categories of social relations frequently involved in seed transactions. These were later quantified in the tracer study . The seed provider categories mentioned here do not constitute an exhaustive list, and each category could be divided into subcategories with overlaps and variations among them. For example, neighbours can sometimes also be relatives or *compadres*. This grouping reflects the informants' own classifications; that is, if an informant referred to a seed provider as an uncle, the provider was classified as a family member, though the person might also be a neighbour.

Family members and acquaintances are the most common sources or recipients of seed. Most seed transactions took place between people who already knew each other and shared a feeling of mutual obligation. Informants in focus group discussions and ethnographic interviews were not able to identify specific persons as particular seed-relations (except for researchers involved in the CIMMYT/INIFAP project, which included a seed distribution activity).

The data regarding social relations do not provide evidence of farmers' involvement in specialized institutions or groups for the mutual supply of seed. *Relationship between social relations and seed transactions* Trust is important for these farmers. Trust in the seed may often derive from a relationship of trust between the recipient and the provider.

The data suggest a systematic relationship between transaction type and supplier-recipient relationship . Inheritance and gifts are the most common transactions among kin. While purchase is common among all social relationships, it isclearly the most common among strangers and acquaintances. It seems that as social distance between supplier and recipient increases, the frequency of purchases increases and the frequency of gifts and inheritance decreases.

In barter and exchange among acquaintances and strangers, informants also said that quantities were calculated based on market prices, but rates in transactionswith kin or a close relationship might be more favourable. Clearly no particular type of transaction is restricted to a single category of seed supplier. Closeness of social relationship improves chances of preferential treatment a finding that is consistent with Sahlin's findings on primitive exchange but it does not determine the type of transaction.In interviews as well as focus group discussions, informants emphasized that seed must be of good quality and appropriate for target production conditions and preferences. Some seed seekers also take into consideration the way the seed has been cultivated and what they know about the general quality of a supplier's work.

The easiest source of knowledge and trustworthy information, not surprisingly, is the people with whom the farmer already has close social relations. Farmers may already know the characteristics of varieties used by kin or close friends, and they can easily obtain more information. Conversations with family members, compadres, and neighbours, as well as observations of what other farmers were growing, were among the most frequently reported ways of obtaining information about seed used elsewhere in the community.

Acquiring seed from trusted sources reduces the risk of obtaining inappropriate seed. Similarly, seed transactions can occur through many types of social relationships, so farmers are not dependent on a single supplier. *Frequencies of seed transactions* It is difficult to assess the frequency of seed transactions. Farmers do not keep records of such transactions, and estimates must rely on the memories of those interviewed.

In the tracer study, seed transactions involving current cultivars were carefully registered, noting the year they took place and allowing farmers to go as far back in time as desired. Recent transactions are more likely to be remembered than those from a long time ago. Notwithstanding these limitations, an estimate of the frequency of seed transactions was calculated.

The distribution between acquisitions and instances of providing seed is approximately the same, meaning that on average acquisitions occur 0.31 times every year and provisions 0.39 times a year (in both cases, approximately once every three years). In 2001 only 24.2 per cent and 20.9 per cent of farmers in the tracer study engaged in seed acquisitions and distributions, respectively. Seed transactions are apparently infrequent and do not involve a large number of farmers every year.

Three parameters were identified to analyze the presence of collective action among farmers to access seed of a diverse set of maize landraces:

1. a group of farmers;
2. rules or practices; and
3. derived benefits.

Within these three parameters, the expected collective action was not found. First, if a farmer is a member of a group related to seed supply, one would have expected informantsto be able to name particular people whom they rely upon to obtainseed time after time. This was not so. In many cases, farmers had trouble remembering the people with whom they had had transactions. While many seed transactions take place within prior existing social relations, most seed transactions do not involve any direct long-term obligations between suppliers and recipients, as would have been expected in a specialized organisation or group. In other words, while individual farmers participate in groups, networks, or other organisations, none of these networks appear to revolve specifically around issues related to seed supply. In fact, it is when farmers experience problems related to seed that they draw on existing networks and social relations to identify possible solutions.

Second, there were many types of seed transactions. The diversity of transactions, even under similar circumstances, as well as their bilateral nature, suggests that there is no fixed procedure or otherwise clearly defined frame collective action in informal seed exchange work for seed transactions, whereas a collective action scenario would involve a set of relatively well-defined practices. Seed needs, and hence transactions, do not seem to have a special status. They appear to be just another resource that farmers occasionally share with each other as part of the arrangements that make life possible in rural areas.

The transactions are not governed by specific seed-related rules but are negotiated in the wider context of the social relation between the involved parties, so the particular details of the transaction may depend on many issues that may not be related specifically to seed.

For example, the seed provider may give favourable treatment to those he considers very close relations, regardless of whether the issue is seed, a request for labour, or the loan of farm implements.

Third, no clear benefit seems to be associated with collective action. Part of the rationale for the original hypothesis was that seed loss was the principal driving force behind seed transactions and that collective action would reduce the problem of seed loss. The results showed that this is not the case—seed loss does not seem to be a major problem for these farmers—and a more important driver for acquiring seed is farmers' experimentation. Clearly experimentation is a form of managing risk to acquire information, but it is related to curiosity and the search for new maize types that fit farmers' needs.

When farmers occasionally do obtain seed from other farmers, it is mainly from close social relations. There are good reasons for this. The cost of obtaining information on different varieties and availability of seed should be relatively low, given that it can be obtained as part of normal, frequent social interactions.

The social ties give rise to trust and confidence that the seed has the desired characteristics and quality. At the same time, farmers often have first-hand knowledge of the varieties grown by relatives or friends. If the variety is grown in the same community under conditions similar to those in the farmer's own fields, uncertainty related to environmental adaptation is reduced. Finally, obtaining seed from a close social relation can often securepreferential treatment in the transaction. Close social relations are an important but not exclusive source of seed for farmers, however. Farmers do get seed from people outside their family circle, particularly through purchase.

This variation in seed sources emphasizes the flexible and sometimes *ad hoc* nature of seed transactions among farmers. Given the low frequency of seed loss, the current seed dynamics, in whicheach farmer maintains and reproduces one or more landraces and only infrequently engages in a seed exchange, appear relatively resilient in terms of maintaining local crop genetic resource diversity.

Nevertheless, these dynamics depend on sufficient opportunities for obtaining seed from others when the need arises. At the moment this does not appear to be a major limitation, but future changes to the production system may alter this. For example, a sharp drop in the number of maize farmers, due to migration or shifting to other crops, could limit the efficacy of the current practices for maize seed acquisition, particularly if individual farmers assume that others are maintaining certain seed types but nobody actually does so.

Farmers generally save seed from one crop cycle to the next. The need to acquire new seed is therefore occasional rather than constant or recurrent. The incentives for collective action may be low because the fixed costs may exceed the benefits, given the relatively low frequency of acquiring seed off of the farm.

Rather than maintaining collective action for seed supply, farmers mobilize social resources on an *ad hoc* basis to solve a problem of seed shortage or to take advantage of an interesting opportunity for accessing new seed.

Farmers' seed management in the study communities entails very low transactions costs, and the seed available through existing social relations is sufficiently reliable to prevent seed loss from being a major problem. Collective action would have to bring very considerable benefits to improve on this.

Within the three parameters identified for examining collective action, this was not found to be an important element in farmers' local seed practices. However, the mobilization of social relations plays a crucial part in relation to farmers' seed transactions, and the types of seed transactions are not random, but should rather be seen as the outcome of a negotiation which in turn may reflect certain rules within a social group.

The way collective action was operationalized here could be considered quite restrictive: it is confined to formal organisations with very strict group membership with the sole purpose of supporting seed flows.

Its advantage, however, is that it provides very specific predictions to test. Even if these are rejected, it provides a rigorous opportunity to learn and reassess the hypothesis and associated assumptions.

One could alternatively consider the existence of more informal institutions with rules that are not predetermined and that adjust to contingencies. These 'fuzzy' rules are more difficult to identify, but they are also more flexible and better suited to deal with risk and uncertainty (for example, crop failure or storage problems). Add to this the desire to experiment. Under these circumstances, it would be reasonable to conclude that elements of collective action in other spheres play an indirect role in seed exchange. One has to be careful, however, not to interpret any outcome of a negotiation in a social group as evidence of collective action, since this could dilute the concept to a degree where almost any activity that is not undertaken in a social vacuum would become a form of collective action.

From a methodological perspective, the findings presented here provide suggestions for other studies regarding collective action. It is important to identify certain minimum criteria to use as indicators for the presence of collective action in a particular context. Furthermore, the specific issue or problem in relation to which collective action is being considered, and the affected population, should be clarified at an early point in the research.

In the initial discussion of the concept of collective action, two approaches were identified: one which is based on the view of collectivities as social entities and another which starts from the perspective of the individual social actor.

This study suggests that the point of departure of further studies of informal seed exchange should be the ways and processes through which individual farmers deal with issues and concerns related to seed and the incentives they face to act individually or collectively.

One can hypothesize that collective action in seed supply may be quite important in circumstances where seed loss is frequent and widespread and where farmers acting as a group may increasetheir individual chance of accessing seed when needed (e.g., areas that suffer frequent, but patchy droughts so that not everybody is affected at the same time), or where there is an interest or need for seed of diverse crop types but information about this diversity may be very difficult to gather, as in environmentally heterogeneous areas with very low population density.

Several other issues also merit further study. For example, if collective action does not play a primary role in the organisation of maize seed dynamics in these communities, then what does? How does informal seed supply actually work? What are the organizing principles that underlie local seed supply and help shape farmers' practices? Likewise, it would be interesting to understand the extent to which issues regarding the availability of and access to seed of a diverse set of maize varieties are perceived as a limiting factor and whether or not they influence farmers' transaction costs in relation to seed acquisition.

An important implication of the findings presented here is the challenge that certain issues would present to the development of a commercial seed sector in this area of Mexico.

The demand for seed from external sources, whether seed of improved or farmer varieties, is small. Furthermore, these farmers have different needs and preferences and therefore require different maize types. One size does not fit all (or at least 'a few sizes do not fit all'). Interventions such as those practiced in the CIMMYT/INIFAP research project demonstrated farmers' interest in acquiring seed of other maize varieties.

As part of that project, farmers purchased seed of many diverse maize varieties, but only in small quantities and for experimentation. As mentioned earlier, 2726 kg of seed were sold to 371 farmers, but the average amount purchased was around 4.3 kg. To sell one ton of seed, almost 250 transactions are required.

This may not be such a problem if the demand is only for one or two varieties, but if the demand is for many different varieties, the costs of selling seed may be too high for a commercial provider. Supplying seed under such circumstances may not be a self-sustaining enterprise, since commercial seed enterprisesmost likely have to supply larger quantities of fewer varieties to be financially viable.

Finally, interventions based on collective action to support farmers' efforts to maintain maize diversity in this region, such as establishing community seed banks, may not be successful. Interventions directed more towards individual farmers, such as the CIMMYT/INIFAP research project, or which build on local institutions that serve other purposes, may be more effective.

11 Agricultural Biodiversity

Agricultural biodiversity is a sub-set of general biodiversity. It includes all forms of life directly relevant to agriculture: rare seed varieties and animal breeds (farm biodiversity), but also many other organisms such as soil fauna, weeds, pests, predators, and all of the native plants and animals (wild biodiversity) existing on and flowing through the farm. However, most attention in this field is given to crop varieties and to crop wild relatives. Cultivated varieties can be broadly classified into "modern varieties" and "farmer's or traditional varieties". Modern varieties are the outcome of formal breeding and are often characterized as 'high yielding'. For example the short straw wheat and rice varieties of the Green Revolution. In contrast, farmer's varieties (also known as landraces) are the product of (breeding and) selection carried out by farmers. Together, these varieties represent high levels of genetic diversity and are therefore the focus of most crop genetic resources conservation efforts. Agricultural biodiversity is the basis of our agricultural food chain, developed and safeguarded by farmers, livestock breeders, forest workers, fishermen and indigenous peoples throughout the world. The use of agricultural biodiversity (as opposed to non diverse production methods) can contribute to food security and livelihood security.

Although the term *agricultural biodiversity* is relatively new - it has come into wide use in recent years as evidenced by bibliographic references - the concept itself is quite old. It is the result of the careful selection and inventive developments of farmers, herders and fishers over millennia. Agricultural biodiversity is a vital sub-set of biodiversity. It is a use of life, i.e. ancillary biotechnologies, by Mankind whose food and livelihood security depend on the sustained management of those diverse biological resources that are important for food and agriculture. As for everything, agricultural biodiversity can be used, not used, misused and even abused. Agricultural biodiversity includes:

- Domesticated rop and 'wild' plants (called: crop wild relatives), including woodland and aquatic plants (used for food and other natural resources based products), domestic and wild animals (used for food, fibre, milk, hides, furs, power, organic fertilizer), fish and other aquatic animals, within field, forest, rangeland and aquatic ecosystems.
- Non-harvested species within production agroecosystems that support food provision, including soil micro-biota, pollinators and so on.
- Non-harvested species in the wider environment that support food production agroecosystems (agricultural, pastoral, forest and aquatic ecosystems).

However, agricultural biodiversity, sometimes called Agrobiodiversity, "encompasses the variety and variability of animals, plants and micro-organisms which are necessary to sustain key functions of the agroecosystem, its structure and processes for, and in support of, food production and food security". It further "comprises genetic, population, species, community, ecosystem, and landscape components and human interactions with all these."

Aquatic diversity is also an important component of agricultural biodiversity. The conservation and sustainable use of local aquatic ecosystems, ponds, rivers, coastal commons by artisanal fisherfolk and smallholder farmers is important to the survival of both humans and the environment. Since aquatic organisms, including fish, provide much of our food supply as well as underpinning the income of coastal peoples, it is critical that fisherfolk and smallholder farmers have genetic reserves and sustainable ecosystems to draw upon as aquaculture and marine fisheries management continue to evolve.

Genetic erosion in agricultural and livestock biodiversity is the loss of genetic diversity, including the loss of individual genes, and the loss of particular combinants of genes (or gene complexes) such as those manifested in locally adapted landraces. The term genetic erosion is sometimes used in a narrow sense, such as for the loss of alleles or genes, as well as more broadly, referring to the loss of varieties or even species. The major driving forces behind genetic erosion in crops are: variety replacement, land clearing, overexploitation of species, population pressure, environmental degradation, overgrazing, policy and changing agricultural systems.

The main factor, however, is the replacement of local varieties by high yielding or exotic varieties or species. A large number of varieties can also often be dramatically reduced when commercial varieties (including GMOs) are introduced into traditional farming systems. Many researchers believe that the main problem related to agro-ecosystem management is the general tendency towards genetic and ecological uniformity imposed by the development of modern agriculture. Pressures for that ecological uniformity on farmers and breeders is caused by the food industry demand for more and more raw materials consistency.

Human Dependency

Agricultural biodiversity is not only the result of human activity but human life is dependent on it not just for the immediate provision of food and other natural resources based goods, but for the maintenance of areas of land and waters that will sustain production and maintain agroecosystems and the wider biological and environmental services (biosphere).

Agricultural Biodiversity provides:

- Sustainable production of food and other agricultural products emphasising both strengthening sustainability in production systems at all levels of intensity and improving the conservation, sustainable use and enhancement of the diversity of all genetic resources for food and agriculture, especially plant and animal genetic resources, in all types of production systems.
- Biological or life support to production emphasising conservation, sustainable use and enhancement of the biological resources that support sustainable production systems, particularly soil biota, pollinators and predators. Ecological and social services provided by agro-ecosystems such as landscape and wildlife protection, soil protection and health (fertility, structure and function), water cycle and water quality, air quality, CO_2 sequestration, etc.

Comparisons of Cropping Systems

The general trend noticed by the analysis of biodiversity present in different cropping systems (e.g., industrial agriculture and organic farming) was that a greater the diversity of crops (temporally and spacially) resulted in a greater overall biodiversity of the agroecosystem, though this is not always the case. A meta-analysis of studies comparing biodiversity noted that, when compared to organic cropping systems, conventional systems had significantly lower species richness and abundance (30% greater richness and 50 per cent greater abundance in organic systems, on average), though 16 per cent of studies did find a greater level of species richness in conventional systems Another study found that cropping systems that required heavy use of chemical amendments (e.g., the widespread broadcasting of pesticides and glyphosate, a practice ubiquitously found throughout the United States and Canada) had significantly greater levels of pollination deficits, whereas organic fields of the same crop (Canola) witnessed no pollination deficits . Other cropping systems like permaculture have undergone little study to determine relative levels of biodiversity compared to other cropping systems, but because they continue to reinforce the goals of increasing overall crop biodiversity, it can be extrapolated that an even greater level of biodiversity would be observed.

Agroecosystems Vs. Natural Ecosystems

Agricultural biodiversity has spatial, temporal and scale dimensions especially at agroecosystem levels. These agroecosystems - ecosystems that are used for agriculture - are determined by three sets of factors: the genetic resources (biodiversity), the physical environment and the human management practices. There are virtually no ecosystems in the world that are "natural" in the sense of having escaped human influence. Most ecosystems have been to some extent modified or cultivated by human activity for the production of food and income and for livelihood security. However there are no places that cannot be returned to the natural landscape.

12 Local Maize Seed Acquisition

Farmers' perceived transaction costs in relation to maize seed acquisition in the Central Valleys of Oaxaca are explored using an ethnographic approach. Issues of information about maize seed, seed transaction negotiation and enforcement are examined from a small-scale farmers' perspective through the use of qualitative data. Findings indicate that farmers' perceived transaction costs are low to negligible in most cases where seed transactions take place locally, and trust is identified as a factor which serves to reduce transaction costs to a minimum. Though not a transaction cost in the conventional economic sense of the term, it is argued that the risk of crop failure, due to inadequate seed, is a major concern for farmers in relation to seed acquisition.

As should be clear by now, most farmers in the study area continue to produce their own maize seed year after year. However, maize farmers do occasionally acquire seed from other sources, mostly other farmers, either because of seed loss due to climatic or storage problems, or because they want to try out or work with other kinds of maize. Previous research in the region showed that 89.7 per cent of maize seed lots were saved by farmers from their ownprevious harvest, and the rest were acquired from other farmers.

These farmers have different needs and require seed of diverse landraces with multiple traits in particular combinations. Finding seed that meets the individual farmer's particular requirements is not always easy

(CIMMYT, 2002). First, the farmer has to find out who grows what maize variety and investigate the characteristics and performance of the maize of interest. Then he/she must make sure that the information offered is trustworthy and the seed is reliable. Finally, he/she has to negotiate the conditions of the transaction with the seed provider. Under such conditions it therefore seemed reasonable to expect that acquisition of seed of diverse maize varieties entails high transaction costs to individual farmers.

The small-scale farmers' perspective may not necessarily appear to be rational and coherent, and it may not fit nicely into a preconceived model of how farmers should consider their reality. We should therefore not be surprised that the findings do not coincide fully with the model we took as a point of departure, that is, the concept of transaction costs as presented in the economic literature.

The term 'transaction costs' has been defined as the costs incurred by participants in an exchange in order to initiate and complete the transactions. Transaction costs are often subdivided into search or information costs (costs of obtaining information about the product and its price as well as about trading partners), negotiation costs (costs of negotiating and carrying out the transaction), andmonitoring or enforcement costs (costs of ensuring the terms of transaction).

Transaction costs are specific to each market participant. As pointed out by researchers this means that there is no single effective market price at which exchanges take place. Furthermore, as argued by researchers, transaction cost issues cannot be understood apart from issues of perception, that is, the perception and definition of reality of the social actors. Therefore, transaction costs are difficult to measure in any objective way.

Here the notion of transaction costs are understood in a broad sense and may include other costs or 'sacrifices' that farmers may have to incur to carry out a seed transaction– even if unsuccessful. These include opportunity costs in terms of time, loss of prestige, risk assumed or others.

The concept of transaction costs is essentially a child of economic theory, although it has also been used by non-economists studying different aspects of economic life. However, the concept of transaction costs does not exist as such in the terminology of ordinary Oaxacan small-scale farmers. As stated above, the ethnographical approach is open and does not define the issues before the study is undertaken.

Instead, this approach seeks to understand the issue from the informant's perspective. As such, the point of departure for this study was to try to identify the costs, sacrifices or concerns, which farmers experience in relation to seed transactions.

Admittedly, this rather nebulous definition may not be sufficient for the purpose of an analysis based on economic theory. However, in as far as our goal is to understand what factors farmers consider a sacrifice in relation to seed acquisition, it is necessary to examine this from a farmer's perspective. In any case, the idea is to look at this from a small-scale farmer's point of view and consider what they consider a cost.

This applies both in the cases where the question is, for instance, about time spent in a particular way, which could have been spent differently, thereby in theory representing a (lost) opportunity; as well as where the question is one of shadow value, for example, by using my own seed, I loose the opportunity of selling it instead. In other words, this is seen as the real cost of using own seed. Most of the farmers interviewed see it as a cost, if they have to acquire seed from someone else, whereas the common perception of using one's own seed is, that it is 'free'. Therefore, notwithstanding that economic theory would look differently at this; from a farmer's perspective, this does not constitute a transaction cost.

Economists may well disagree with this perspective; however, within an ethnographical framework there is no other way to address this.

Observed – Unobserved Costs

Transactions with the formal seed sector in the study region are few and far between, which means that it has not been possible to study this in any great detail, as the study was carried out with a limited number of informants. The unobserved costs, that is, of formal seed sector transactions or non-local transactions, could potentially be relatively high; however, at this point in time data is not available to document this. In a quantitative survey with many informants this may be approached more easily.

The transaction costs are related to the costs of obtaining the 'desired good'. It could be argued that the desired good is a 'bagful of maize seed'. However, the farmer is not looking for seed *per se*, but rather for an input in the crop production cycle. In that sense the desired product is a successful harvest which yields grain and fodder of the desired quality.

In relation to seed acquisitions, therefore, the farmer wants seed that will perform successfully underthe production conditions present in a particular field, and which produces maize grain with the particular qualities desired by the farmer, for instance in terms of consumption qualities, storageability or marketing.

However, farmers know that simply by looking at the seed, it is not possible to tell under which conditions, it will perform well or if it will germinate at all – in other words, seed is not transparent here). When acquiring seed, if the farmer is uncertain as to whether it will live up to the expectations mentioned above, he/she runs the risk that the acquired good may not actually be the desired good. The problem is that the farmer will not know this until he/she plants the seed. In the following this is referred to as the problem of inadequate seed. It should be noted that this can mean either maize seed that is not adapted to the given environmental or managementcircumstances, or, seed which produces maize that lacks the particular consumption characteristics the farmer sought at the moment of acquiring the seed. From an economic point of view, we may want to separate the seed transaction from the rest of the production process, but for the farmer these are inseparable; he or she does not procure seed unless it is with the specific purposeof obtaining a harvest.

Furthermore, the farmers correctly draw attention to the fact that the problem of inadequate seed arises in the moment of acquiring the seed, and not at some later stage in the crop production cycle. As such, both from a farmer's point of view as well as from an economic point of view, It would argue that the risk of crop failure due to inadequate seed should be considered a transaction cost - in the same way that the risk of gettingthe wrong product due to lack of information would be considered a transaction cost. Meanwhile, it should be kept in mind that crop failure may also be caused by a series of other factors, such as drought, pests, disease or other, in which case it would be a production cost.

Search Costs

In general, searching for information is a situation in which farmers draw on their various social networks. Access to information is heavily influenced by the nature of the farmer's networks of social relations including his/her social and political standing or connectedness. Physical isolation can also influence the flow of information, in other words, the further away from the village the smaller the flow of information.

In several respects this is the case of Francisco and the other farmers in Rio Blanco who live and farm in the hills several hours travel from the village of San Pablo Huitzo. Still, much also depends on the personality and skills of the individual farmer. For example, despite her socially and economically marginal position, Miriam Almost all farmers at some stage engage in some kind of informal experimentation. Some farmers are more persistent and structured in their experimentation than others, and those who are continuously on the look-out for new and interesting things may be more curious and innovative than the majority. This is not determined by age or economic standing.

Rather, it seems to depend mostly on people's personalities. However, it should be noted, that poverty is often accompanied by risk aversion, and that very poor farmers therefore may be somewhat more reluctant to engage in experiments that imply risk, or, their experiments may be of a more humble, low cost nature.

Many farmers in the study communities like to carry out their own experiments, trying out seed of different crops and crop varieties. When farmers come across interesting maize material, they will often try it out on a small piece of land first, either in the field or in the backyard. Depending on the experiment's outcome and the circumstances in general, they will then decide whether or not to plant this material again on a larger piece of land. Experimentingallows farmers to see for themselves how the variety performs and if it is convenient for them, without incurring major risks of failure if the variety does not perform.

In general maize farmers in the Central Valleys believe that if a maize variety performs well under certain agro-ecological conditions, it may not necessarily perform equally well under different conditions - what breeders call a high genotype-by-environment interaction.

Seed Quality

Seed quality is affected by a range of factors (e.g. free from damage by pests and diseases, age, and appropriate storage), which all have a bearing on the viability of the seed. At the end of the day it all comes down to the ability ofthe seed to germinate. In terms of seed quality, this is what counts at the farmer's level.

As mentioned above, seed is not transparent - one cannot know the traits and performance of the plants that will grow from it merely by looking at the seed before planting. By looking at the seed, farmers can check immediately observable features, including physical damage to the seed, but apart from this, seed quality can be difficult to determine. Age, pathogens, or inappropriate storage may affect germination; however, this is not necessarily visible to the human eye, and though farmers usually inspect the seed before acquisition, in these regards farmers in the Central Valleys must rely on the information given to them by the seed provider.

Farmer Seed Criteria: Clean and Undamaged

From a biological point of view any healthy maize kernel could serve as seed or as food. However, farmers in the Central Valleys distinguish between seed and grain, seed being a specially selected category consisting only of 'best quality' maize kernels (large uniform size, clean and undamaged by pests or other agents), whereas grain is a mixed category, albeit with a certain minimum quality control enforced at the time of de-husking.

To a certain extent the criteria behind farmers' definition of seed (specially selected, large uniform seed, clean, undamaged by insects or other) protect against some of the factors that may affect germination.

For example, all farmers stressed that the seed must be clean and intact, that is, it should not be stained or show any signs of mould and it should not be damaged by insects. In the latter case, explains Pablo H., the seed will not germinate. He adds that when inspecting seed, he breaks one to see if the '*puntito*' [pointy end] is intact. In the opposite case, or if the seed disintegratesby itself, it is no good, he explains. Some farmers are aware that the age of the seed can affect germination. Some years ago, Pablo H. acquired a small quantity of hybrid maize seed through SAGARPA (Secretaría de Agricultura, Ganadería, Desarrollo Rural, Pescay Alimentación). He did not use it all, and when five years later he planted what was left over of the seed, it did not germinate. Don Pablo reflects on this and comments: In the stores where they sell [seed], it sometimes happens that they have already had it stored there for a long time. That is when this sort of thing can happen. They buy in big quantities, so they sometimes have some left over. He mentions that this happened to him on another occasion, not with maize, but with onion seed. After much arguing with the stockistwho had sold him the seed, he was compensated with another tin of onion seed.

Although farmers inspect the seed before acquiring it, thereby limiting the chance of bad seed quality, this does not provide a guarantee that the seed will germinate. In various regards, farmers must still rely on the information given by the seed provider and depend on its trustworthiness. This constitutes an important reason for farmers to prefer to acquire seed from somebody they know and trust.

The Maize Mill

The maize mill is another forum where farmers learn who has what types of maize. Women gather here every day, each one bringing her *nixtamal* (cooked maize ready for milling). While each one waits for her turn, the time is spent talking and meanwhile the various *nixtamals* of different kinds of maize can be admired and the quality of the dough can be assessed as it is milled and gathered.

In the following, an overview of the transaction costs related to small-scale farmers' maize seed acquisitions is pulled together, based on the findings presented in the previous sections. This is followed by an overview of the risk factors, which farmers perceive in relation to maize seed acquisitions. Farmers' strategies for risk reduction in relation to maize seed acquisitions are then discussed, and finally an overview of the cost factors related to the acquisition of different categories of seed is presented.

The findings presented in the previous sections show that the easiest source of knowledge and trustworthy information about seed, not surprisingly, is the people whom the farmer already knows and trusts. Often he or she may already know the characteristics of varieties used by kin or close friends and can easily obtain more information. Indeed, the most frequent ways of obtaining information about maize seed from outside the household are:

- Farmer experimentation;
- Conversations with family members, *compadres*, and neighbours;
- Paying attention to what other farmers are growing and how it performs (e.g. when working together in a *tequio* or a *guelaguetza*; and moving around in the communities);
- Furthermore, farmers usually inspect the seed before acquisition as a minimum measure of protection against low seed quality.

In general these ways of acquiring information about maize seed are not interpreted by farmers as sacrifices. Rather, to a great extent, they form part of every day social practice and conversation and are normally not separated from ordinary social life. Still, if the information or the seed is sought further away, for instance in Oaxaca, it may entail a cost. However, when farmers go to the market or travel to the city, they always take advantage of the occasion to combine several tasks, thereby economizing on transaction costs.

When looking for seed, farmers will refer each other to seed providers they know and trust. Referral by others may imply costs in terms of increased search time and the social relations with the new person might be less close.

This in turn may lead to increased costs in the sense that the one who obtains seed may not get the preferential treatment, which could have occurred with a closer relation. On the other hand the new contact may represent an expansion of one's social network.

Farmers' negotiation costs in relation to maize seed acquisition, as reported in this study, are generally low and mostly consist of the time and effort spent to achieve a satisfactory transaction. The type of social relation between the parties involved may influence the outcome of the negotiation, that is, the type of transaction or the price and form of payment. Similarly, depending on the circumstances, the reputation of either of the parties may influence thenegotiation, positively or negatively. Furthermore, farmers sometimes try to haggle the price of seed. This way the financial cost of the seed may be reduced; however, depending on the situation, this could be outweighed by increased negotiation costs, in terms of social responsibility or loss of prestige on behalf of the person acquiring the seed.

In terms of enforcement costs the situation is similar. The possibility of compensation, for example in the case of low germination, is generally very low. The vast majority of seed transactions in the study area are informal and in most cases the farmer has little or no means of actual enforcement. As a result it is essentially presumed that the seed receiver assumes the risk. Nevertheless, a few examples were found of compensation for seed that did not germinate.

In these cases, however, the compensation only covered the seed itself, not the investment in land preparation and loss of harvest, that is, only a very partial compensation. Still, if a transaction is not completed satisfactorily, there may be other repercussions. The seed seeker may avoid that particular seed provider in future and not recommend him/her to others, or; if the fault is on the seed receiver's side, the seed provider may be very reluctant to engagein new seed transactions with this person.

Transactions are normally considered to be finalized when payment is completed. However, regardless of the type of transaction, farmers often look at seed transactions from a perspective of mutual favours and consideration. In this light, most informants, if not all, agree that one ought to return the favour, if the need arises and one has the opportunity to do so.

This can be interpreted in the sense that, although the transaction has been finalized, a relationship of mutual help and reciprocity continues or has been initiated. In this context certain obligations may pertain, although they are not clearly spelt out. This, on the other hand, permits flexibility and practical solutions whenever problems arise and social networks of mutual help are called upon. Given the definition of transaction costs as the costs incurred by participants in order to initiate and complete a transaction, it could be argued that the issue of risk connected to crop failure or germination failure is not part of thetransaction, but rather represents risks strictly inherent in farming. Thus, it could be argued, these issues should be regarded as production costs, and not as transaction costs.

However, many farmers have experienced crop failure, either as partial or complete harvest losses for different reasons. When acquiring seed from outside the farm, the risk of crop failure due to inadequate seed is therefore interpreted as a 'real' risk and constitutes a serious concern for farmers. Furthermore, to a large extent, the risk of crop failure due to inadequate seed is directly linked to the lack of transparency of seed. On one hand, there is the issue of seed quality, that is, the question of whether the seed will germinate. On the other hand, if it germinates there is still the question of how the genotype will perform under the particular agro-ecological and management conditions, and whether it will display the traits and characteristics demanded by the farmer.

The question of seed quality mainly implies a transaction cost in terms of risk of germination failure. However, as long as the seed is acquired from another farmer within the same community, the issue of seed quality does not seem to invoke any notion of transaction costs among the informants. In general, as long as the seed was clean and undamaged, farmers in both communities had difficulty imagining that locally acquired seed would not germinate.

That is, in this situation the perceived transaction costs in terms of germination failure were very low or zero. This may increase in the cases where grain is used as seed, as grain is often stored with less care than seed and though the selection is careful, deficiencies in storage may have lowered seed quality.

Meanwhile, informants manifested a general distrust in market vendors and maize seed from these or other unknown sources. In that sense, the moment farmers acquire seed from unknown sources, for example, from outside the community, transaction costs increase drastically in terms of perceived insecurity regarding seed quality and/or seed traits, in other words, risk of crop failure due to inadequate seed. The non-transparency of seed creates problems of incomplete and/or asymmetric information. The seed provider may know that the seed performs well under the usual conditions where he or she has planted it. However, these conditions may be different from the conditions in the seed receiver's field, and the information may therefore not be applicable.

Likewise, the seed receiver normally knows the place where the seed will be planted, but this knowledge may not be sufficiently comparable to the knowledge of the seed supplier. In both cases, the asymmetry in information may lead to the acquisition of inadequate seed. Thus it is not necessarily due to ill will on behalf of the seller - it may simply be attributed to incomplete information on the local production conditions or incomplete information on the requirements of the seed receiver in terms of seed traits.

The problem of asymmetry of information is less when seed provider and seed receiver are from the same area. In that case the chances are high, that the seed receiver will know the circumstances the seed was produced under, and likewise, that the seed provider will know the kind of production conditions the seed receiver requires the seed for. However, when distances increase,it may accentuate the problem of asymmetry of information, as thechances are that each one will know less about the conditions in which the other grows his/her maize.

Other types of risk may also constitute transaction costs in relation to seed transactions. For example, in the case of exchange or lending, the seed provider assumes a transaction cost in terms of the risk of not receiving the expected quality of seed in return. For lending there is furthermore a time factor, which can be interpreted as negative or positive: the lender is without his/her seed for a time, but on the other hand he/she receives fresh seed in return. Finally, there is yet another risk factor for the lender; that of the seed not being returned. Depending on the amount of seed in question, this can be a relatively high cost, and according to informants' testimonies this is the main reason for seed providers' reluctance to use this type of transaction.

As pointed out in the findings, informal experimentation provides farmers with first hand information about the characteristics and the performance of particular maize types under specific agro-ecological and management circumstances.

Upon evaluating the experiment, the farmer has a relatively good basis for deciding whether the maize type in question is appropriate in relation to his or her production objectives. Such experimentation typically implies planting a separate variety at a reduced scale (e.g. 1-2 rows) but according to the farmers who participated in this study, it does not represent a significant cost, for example, in terms of extra time or labour. The principal cost is the risk that the experiment will not be successful. However, this is manageable due to the small scale of most farmer experiments. Furthermore, at the end of the day the carrying out of small-scale experiments reduces the risk of major failure. Farmer experiments therefore serve both the purpose of information and of risk control.

Strictly speaking, there may be a question of transaction costs in terms of time linked to farmer experimentation in the sense that the time used gathering information is prolonged. However, for most small-scale farmers in the Central Valleys of Oaxaca, the time spent carrying out farmer experiments is not a significant transaction cost in comparison to the risks implied, if he/she had decided not to do the testing on a small piece of land first.

Furthermore, experiments which are normally established with relatively small amounts of seed, are often used by farmers to multiply seed. If the farmer chooses to continue to plant that particular maize variety, he/she may decide to use the kernels harvested in the 'experiment' as seed, thereby avoiding the need to acquire seed again.

Trust is a key issue in seed transactions. This is directly related to the lack of transparency of seed. The findings indicate that seed acquired from people the farmer knows and trusts, in general is perceived as entailing less risk of crop failure due to inadequate seed, than seed acquired from unknown sources. In other words, the more the seed receiver knows and trusts the seedprovider, the less the perceived risk related to incomplete or asymmetric information. Acquiring seed from trusted social relations can therefore be seen as a way of reducing the problem of lack of transparency in seed, which in turn reduces transaction costs in terms of perceived risk of crop failure due to inadequate seed. Relations of trust are conducive to easy access and exchange of information at low costs.

Acquiring seed through relations of trust may also enhance one's possibilities of preferential treatment: for example, in terms of the type of transaction, such as lending or exchange, which are almost exclusively carried out between people with prior social relations of trust, instead of purchase. However, in the case of asymmetrical relations, preferential treatment may occasionally come at a social cost in terms of the confirmation or reinforcement of the difference in status of the parties involved (e.g. where one person is dependent on the other).

The issue of trust may be influenced by either of the contracting parties' reputations. For example, acquiring seed to try out something new / experiment is accepted as a normal farming activity, as is the occasional complementation of seed. However acquiring seed every year, for want of practicing traditional seed selection and saving one's own seed, or, for lack of ability to save seed, easily earns one a reputation of being a lazy/poorly skilled farmer.

This, in turn, is likely to influence the general perception of one's trustworthiness as well as the possibilities for preferential treatment. Nobody wants to lend or exchange seed with someone who is not likely to get a good crop, or who cannot be trusted to fulfil his part of the deal. If the seed seeker is rumoured to be unreliable or not a good farmer, any transaction is therefore likely to be a purchase, unless the seed provider feels a special obligation (e.g. is close kin or *compadre*). On the other hand, the seed supplier may achieve a negative reputation if the seed he /she provided to someone turns out to be of bad quality, or if the seed receiver feels wronged in any other way. This canbe a problem for a commercial seed trader, but also for a farmer acting as seed provider. Interestingly the 'good farmer' appears in general to be trusted much more than the seed trader, who could be argued to have a professionalreputation to protect. This lack of trust in commercial seed merchants couldbe a major barrier for the establishment of a commercial seed sector and theintroduction of new varieties in the region.

When farmers in the study communities acquire maize seed from other farmers, they generally choose the seed provider among the people they trust. As is clear in several of the testimonies cited above, they do not believe that seed acquired in this way, would not be good. This can be interpreted as an expression of generalized trust or social capital as a 'stock' of trust in a group. However, many of the farmers will furthermore possess social capital in the form of 'an individual asset' or personalized trust established through repeated interpersonal interactions with their peers. Therefore, as far as seed transactions within the local community are concerned, it could be argued that both typesof social capital are at work.

Meanwhile, the perceived risk of crop failure due to inadequate seed appears to be relatively high in seed acquired from commercial seed providers, be it agro-veterinary stockists, market vendors or petty commerce shopkeepers.

The remarks and testimonies expressing farmers' distrust of commercial seed providers, makes an example of a situation in which there is neither personalized trust through interpersonal relationships, for example in the form of a previous record of transactions together; nor generalized trust. In fact it is almost the opposite, namely, a belief that the commercial seed seller will do anything to make a profit, including cheating. In other words, while local seed supply can be understood as facilitated by a high degree of both generalized and personalized trust, commercial seed sellers suffer from a general lack of trust. Furthermore, due to farmers' attachment to local maize varieties and the common practice of selecting and saving seed from one's own harvest, seed acquisition from other sources, such as commercial seed sellers, is relatively infrequent. This makes it difficult for individual commercial seed merchants to build up trust through repeated interpersonal interaction.

Others have taken a different perspective on social capital, as discussed in For example, Portes sees social capital as the capacity of individuals to use networks in order to mobilize resources. However, in this particular case where the focus is on transaction costs, it is difficult to distinguish - and makes little difference - whether social capital is permanently present or if it is only brought into play in the transaction. With either view (Fafchamps' or Portes') the conclusion is that social capital significantly reduces the risksinvolved in seed transactions.

In the examples used above, transaction costs consist mainly of an element of risk. However, there seems to be a clear relation between the level of trust in the relationship between the two parties and the risks perceived by the seed receiver, that is, the level of transaction costs.

If the seed provider is from outside the community and a stranger to the seed receiver, meaning there is neither generalized nor personalized trust, the transaction costs in terms of perceived risk are high. On the other hand, if the seed provider is a farmer from the same community as the seed receiver and maybe furthermore a close social relation of his/hers, the level of trust may be high and the transaction costs low.

There seems to be a similar relation between transaction costs in terms of risk on one hand and local seed versus introduced seed, on the other hand, that is, seed that was not acquired from another farmer in the same community To a large degree these perspectives coincide with Plattner's conclusion that the poorer the information, the higher the transaction costs, the riskier the exchange and the more valuable to invest in personalized relationships, which in this case would mean acquiring seed from people one knows and trusts.

Researcher distinguishes between impersonal and personal modes of exchange. An impersonal mode occurs when transactors have no relation with each other beyond the short term of the exchange; and the personal mode refers to transactions between people who have a relationship that endures past the exchange. We could also look at the latter as transactions embedded in people's networks of social relations When transactions are carried out in a personal mode of exchange, the seed recipient hedges the risk of receiving poor seed against the whole social relation with the seedprovider, thus the problem of establishing trust solely based on seed transactions is overcome.

In principle, this would also mean less asymmetry between provider and receiver than in an ordinary market exchange, that is, relatively low transactions costs when acquiring seed within one's own community. The question is, whether this would apply equally to all farmers in the community?

Hardly any of the persons interviewed are completely without any social relations. Still, this does not mean they are all equally well 'connected' or can draw on equal resources in this respect. Nevertheless, for the farmers who are marginalized in one or several ways and are less well connected than others in their community, it is often, albeit not in all cases, even more difficult, troublesome and costly to engage in non-local transactions. If one's Spanish is very poor, if one is illiterate and has difficulty managing numbers, and if on top of that one has to travel a long way for non-local seed transactions, local seed transactions still have many comparative advantages, although it may be more difficult for some than for other people in the same community.

The findings suggest that these costs are negligible in most seed transactions, as long as these take place within the village and farmers' social networks. In this case, no evidence was found of specific investments related to obtaining information, and the negotiation costs are generally smal, though they may increase in the case where the receiver of seed is trying to obtain preferential treatment such as a lower price than normal.

This benefit could then be argued to outweigh the increased negotiation cost. Enforcement costs are not considered relevant as, essentially, it is presumed that the seed receiver assumes the risk. Farmers therefore generally do not expect compensation for crop failure, even though a few examples were found of compensation for seed that did not germinate. However, in these cases the compensation only covered the seed itself, not the investment in land preparation and loss of harvest. It was therefore only a very partial compensation.

In general, the information costs, negotiation costs and enforcement costs in the current seed transactions appear to be negligible or not relevant, and it would be very difficult to quantify these, as originally planned.

The risk of crop failure due to inadequate seed appears to be the main cost in relation to seed transactions. The problem can arise from two sources: either the seed is of poor quality and fails to germinate, or the germplasm is not adequate for the local environment and fails to yield adequately.

Therefore, specifically related to the seed acquisition as such, the question is not whether or not the harvest will fail due to weather conditions, pest attacks or other. Rather, when acquiring seed the farmer's question is: 'Will this seed produce plants, which will perform successfully under the specific condition in my field, and will they produce maize that live up to the standards we expect in my household?' From this perspective, it may be beneficial to treat the issue here referred to as risk of crop failure due to inadequate seed quality or genotype x environment interaction, as a question of quality of information. This could also include the case of maize which turns out not to have the desired characteristics, for example with regard to consumption. In any case, a quantification of transaction costs should include the perceived risk of crop failure due to inadequate seed with regards to seed quality and genotype-byenvironment interaction problems.

Trust and other elements of social capital play a key role in this system and serve to reduce transaction costs to a minimum. Trust as well as social and moral obligations create an environment that is conducive to relatively easy seed transactions. Furthermore, since farmers mostly produce their own maize seed and only acquire seed from other sources once in a while, the system works well. As seed providers, farmers from the same community are considered very trustworthy, and it is regarded as almost impossible that they would supply poor quality seed or provide inadequate information in relation to the seed.

Transaction costs are high however, if a farmer wants to acquire seed outside his or her social network and community; particularly in terms of search costs and risk of crop failure due to inadequate seed. This is further emphasized by the fact that seed providers who are motivated by profit, suchas commercial vendors at the markets and agricultural stockists, often are not regarded as trustworthy. In fact, they are widely suspected of being willing to sell anything without much scruple. From a commercial seed sector point of view, a key problem in the system described here is that small-scale farmers' seed transactions often involve small quantities of seed and are relatively infrequent. In other words, it is not a regularly recurring event.

Furthermore, many of these farmers require diverse maize varieties with different combinations of traits and quality characteristics and seem to be willing to pay only twice the price of maize grain for maize seed. Under these circumstances it is difficult for a commercial seed sector to develop and for individual seed merchants to build, through repeated interpersonal interactions, the trust required to be successful. For a commercial merchant the costs of selling seed of many diverse varieties, on an occasional basis and in relatively small quantities, are likely to be very high. With regards to enhancing farmers' access to seed of diverse maize varieties in terms of 'foreign' varieties, it would seem important to assess not only the transaction costs faced by the purchasers of seed, but also those faced by sellers who can bring interesting new varieties from the outside, but who are motivated by profit rather than social or moral obligations.

13 Farmer's Seed Practices

With the point of departure rooted in an overall actor-oriented approach, a number of analytical concepts and perspectives have been introduced and subsequently applied to various kinds of empirical findings, as part of the challenge of describing and analysing the dynamics of local maize seed practices from a farmer perspective.

Empirically, the objective has been to contribute to an increased understanding of the workings of local seed practices, in order to provide a relevant input to the debate on crop genetic resources and smallholder farmers' access to seed with interesting and desirable characteristics. At the same time, my goal has been to contribute to the debate concerning the relevance of the social sciences to agricultural research and development through the application of a series of analytical perspectives from socio-economics to farmers' seed practices.

The analysis has focused on four main issues, including:

- Farmer's seed practices as a form of local knowledge;
- The role of collective action in relation to the conservation of maize genetic diversity and local seed supply;
- The social organisation of seed supply; and
- Farmers' perceived transaction costs in relation to seed acquisition.

Seed is a key input in crop-based farming everywhere. In addition to being the basis for the majority of the world's agricultural production, it is also a fundamental source of germplasm for crop improvement. Access to seed with desirable characteristics is thus an essential issue for farmers and of major importance for society in order to achieve food security.Local practices for seed management and exchange remain the basis for seed supply for the majority of farmers in developing countries, and many studies have stressed their importance. Many farmers value local crop genetic resources and make special use of diverse crop varieties in their production systems. Decisions regarding varietal choice often depend on multiple considerations, not just yield.

In Mexico, which is a centre of domestication and genetic diversity for maize, farmers continue to play a key role in the maintenance and evolution of this diversity. In the Central Valleys of Oaxaca in Southern Mexico, the structure and evolution of maize genetic diversity depend on a combination of gene flow and farmers' selection. While gene flow allows new genes to enter the local pool of crop genetic diversity, farmers' seed selection, which is strongly influenced by local preferences and culture, allows for the differentiation between varieties from the same farmer or between farmers.

The dynamics of farmers' seed supply practices have important implications, both for the conservation of crop genetic resources on-farm and for the design and implementation of interventions to support conservation. Moreover, in a broader perspective they also have important implications for the introduction of new varieties and seed sector development.

Nevertheless, farmers do occasionally use grain as seed. Therefore, although a clearly defined concept of seed exists (selected, clean, and of good quality), it is not rigid or static. Rather, the concept of seed is dynamic and negotiable, depending on the circumstances. This demonstrates the flexibility in farmers' categories and inclination towards experimentation and practical solutions.

The lack of transparency in seed means that the traits and performance of the plants that will grow from it cannot be assessed by merely looking at the seed. As noted several times, this plays an important role in seed transactions.

With regard to traits and consumption characteristics, environmental adaptation, and seed quality, farmers therefore depend largely on the quality of the information offered by the seed provider. This included elements related to the ambiguity of local concepts and terminologies with multiple meanings, and the differences between performative versus propositional or verbalized knowledge.

The various and rather 'fuzzy' local concepts of seed and variety, and practices such as mixing and complementing seed, served to exemplify the flexibility and negotiability of local concepts. It also served to demonstrate that rather than definitions in terms of clearly stated meanings, concepts, in this perspective, are 'dynamic mental representations'. They may vary from one person to another, and may continue to evolve in response to people's diverse experiences.

Farmers' seed management practices constituted another example of ambiguous categories and the difficulty of expressing performative knowledge in a verbalized form. Similarly, it was pointed out that farmers' experimentation can be seen as an acquisition of first hand information based on performative knowledge rather than just verbalized knowledge. As such, it constitutes a more comprehensive knowledge, which is readily incorporated into the farmers' existing stock of farming knowledge and practices.

It is not surprising that such ambiguity and poly-semic terminology, as well as the problems related to verbalized versus performative knowledge, challenge anyone who attempts to capture and describe farmers' seed practices. In the worst case, failure to recognize this may lead to serious misinterpretations and failure to understand farmers' knowledge and practices. However, if one is aware of the differences between local and scientific knowledge, includingthe aspects of ambiguity influencing local concepts and the issues surrounding performative versus verbalized knowledge, this may further the scientific enquiry. In addition this awareness underlines local knowledge as the driving force in development processes and emphasizes that the challenge for scientific knowledge is to achieve synergies with this - not the other way around.

Using Own Seed

The foundation of maize seed supply in the study communities is farmers' practice of selecting seed from the previous harvest and saving it for the next planting season. Of the farmers who participated in the seed flow tracer study, 75.8 per cent relied entirely on their own seed in 2001. Furthermore, researcher reported that approximately 90 per cent of all seed lots in the study communities were selected by farmers from the previous harvest, while the rest were acquired almost entirely from other farmers.

Once seed is selected and safely set aside, one can rest assured that the seed for the next planting season is secured. Furthermore, the seed will be available when it is needed so the farmer will not incur planting delays. One can therefore avoid spending money and/or time acquiring seed at the last moment before planting, which is when prices typically increase and many households are struggling to raise the means necessary for land preparation and planting.

Farmers' seed selection practices in the study area reflect both the genotypeby- environment consideration and the issue of seed security: knowing the performance of the plants the seed came from, farmers select maize seed according to a set of characteristics that they perceive as favourable in terms of their own particular needs. Due to social, cultural, and environmental conditions, a variety that is appropriate for one farmer may not necessarily be appropriatefor another.

Hence, what better option to fit one's needs and preferences than using the seed that one knows and has selected? Moreover, for some of these farmers, their own maize seed is associated with a certain affection value. This aspect surfaced many times during individual interviews, but was also brought up by farmers during focus group discussions. Seed is often inherited, passed on from parents to children when the latter start farming independently. Often, the seed has been in the family for many years during which it has provided sustenance for the family, whereby it has acquired an inherent affection or symbolic value. Thus, for many farmers in the Central Valleys, the maize seed lot is something theyhave in trust, which links them with previous generations, and which they, in turn, must pass on to their descendants.

In their own way, each of the above mentioned aspects is part of what constitutes the local concept of 'a good farmer', a notion which can be said to lay out certain principles for what is considered appropriate behaviour of a good farmer. This should not be understood in a fixed or prescriptive sense, but rather as a set of guidelines open to individual interpretation and negotiation. One aspect of appropriate behaviour of a 'good farmeris to take good care of his/her seed.

As the female farmers in one of the focus groups stated: [losing seed] is like hurting one's pride in being a good farmer it is like a humiliation! On the other hand, , it appears to be acceptable and legitimate to obtain seed from other farmers in a bad year or for experimentation, provided one is generally thought to manage seed with appropriate care. In this case, the seed receiver has a justifiable need for the seed, and is not someone who prefers to rely onothers rather than make the effort of selecting and storing seed from the previous harvest. In other words, this person 'deserves' the seed and will appreciate the favour.

Clearly, for farmers in the study area, selecting and saving seed is not just a question of saving money, but a decision that has cultural, economic, and agroecological components.

It has been pointed out that, although farmers select their own seed year after year, they may also, occasionally, substitute entirely, complement, or mix their own seed with seed from external sources. Initially a farmer would state: However, further conversation would reveal that on one or more occasions the seed was complemented or mixed with external seed. These practices have also been noted by researcher and from other regions in Mexico. Over time, these and other management practices, for example, how the farmer selects seed, as well as naturally occurring pollen flow from other farmers' maize fields, may well change the genetic make-up of his/her maize.

Although saving seed from one's own harvest is the backbone of local seed supply in the study area, farmers do acquire seed from other sources from time to time.

The quantity of seed involved in farmer-to-farmer seed transactions is often quite small, in many cases less than 8 kg, which according to local standards is what is needed to plant approximately half a hectare . The number of seed acquisitions involving small or very small amounts of maize seed suggests that many of these acquisitions are for the purpose of farmer experimentation, or to complete the amount of seed needed, for example, in case of partial seed loss.

It is difficult to assess the frequency of seed transactions. As explained earlier farmers do not keep records of such transactions, and estimates must rely on the memory of those interviewed. Despite this challenge an estimate of the frequency of farmers' maize seed transactions was calculated based on the data from the seed-flow tracer study.

Seed transactions per farmer were found to be relatively infrequent, occurring on average once every three years .seed transactions were bilateral and took place in diverse ways, even under similar circumstances. No particular procedure or framework for seed transactions was found, as would be expected in the case of collective action. Seed transactions did not appear tostand out against farmers' other dealings, favours or mutual help, but seemed to be negotiated on a case-by-case basis in the wider context of the social relation between the involved parties. Thirdly, despite the expectations underlying the hypothesis, no clear benefits associated with collective action in relation to maize seed supply were identified. Seed loss was found to be occasional rather than constant or recurrent.

At the same time, since most farmersselect and save seed from the previous harvest, generally putting aside more seed than they expect to need for their own planting, the challenge of obtaining seed in the case of seed loss appeared to be less of a problem than originally expected. Instead of investing time and effort in maintaining collective action for a specific problem which only happens occasionally, the maize farmers in the study area address problems of seed shortage or opportunitiesfor accessing new interesting seed on a case-by-case basis. In this regard, the mobilization of social relations was found to play an important part in local seed transactions.

Farmers' Transaction Costs in Relation to Seed Acquisition

Similar to the examination of the role of collective action the study aimed to identify the factors that influence farmers' transaction costs in relation to seed transactions. This also built on an underlying hypothesis, which was not confirmed by the findings, namely that maize seed acquisitions would entail high transaction costs for individual farmers in the study area.

This turned out not to be the case. In fact, transaction costs in relation to maize seed acquisitions were low to negligible in most cases. This was found to be closely linked to the fact that most maize seed transactions in the study area take place among people who know andtrust each other, or, alternatively, at least are from the same community. This makes for an information rich context, often complemented by relations of trust. Under these circumstances information and negotiation costs were described by farmers as minimal. On the other hand, in the situations where farmers acquire seed from unknown seed providers outside their own community, the context of the seed transaction is not as information rich. In addition, commercial seed vendors are sometimes suspected of being untrustworthy.

Under these circumstances, farmers' transaction costs in relation to maize seed acquisitions tend to increase. According to local practice, farmers normally do not expect compensation in the event that the acquired seed does not possess the hoped-for quality orcharacteristics. It is generally presumed that by deciding to accept seed for planting from another party of his/her own choice, the receiver of the seed as sumes the risk. From a farmer perspective, therefore, the issue of enforcement costs is hardly relevant.

Meanwhile, farmers' main concern in relation to maize seed acquisition, in particular with regards to seed acquisition from unknown, non-local sources, was found to be the perceived risk of crop failure due to inadequate seed. Regardless of the reason, crop failure or risk thereof would normally be considered as pertaining to the production process, and therefore not to be a transaction cost.

However, in relation to reflections on the nature of the desired good in seed transactions, and due to the problems associated with the lack of transparency in seed, I have argued that in relation to seed acquisition farmers' perceived risk of crop failure due to inadequate seed should be treated as a problem of insufficient or asymmetric information. Essentially this is an example of the risk of getting the wrong product because of lack of information. Assuming this risk is a sacrifice for the farmer in search of seed. This can be a serious issue for individual farmers, and it should therefore be considered, when assessing the factors that influence farmers' seed acquisition strategies.

Seed Transactions and Social Relations

In this analysis of the dynamics of local seed practices among farmers in the Central Valleys of Oaxaca, I have shown that farmers' maize seed transactions are embedded in concrete contexts, including networks of social relations.

Social networks affect the flow and the quality of information to a significant degree. At the same time they constitute an importantsource of reward and punishment, which often has a bigger impact when coming from others personally known and whose acceptance we seek. Finally, as researcher pointed out, the emergence of trust takes place in the context of social networks.

The presence of trust can provide a more secure environment for transactions and social exchange. Researchers, have demonstrated that uncertainty about product characteristics or performance quality leads people to prefer sellers with whom they have non-commercial ties. This embeds the exchange in a web of obligations and holds the seller's network hostage to appropriate role performance in the economic transaction.

In addition exchange frequency reduces the extent of within-network exchanges that is, network relations are mostly used in connection with notso- frequent acquisitions/ transactions.

In the present study, farmers obtained maize seed from many types of seed providers (e.g. family members, *compadres*, neighbours, friends, acquaintances, strangers, and others). However, the large majority of seed transactions were found to take place between people who know each other prior to the seed transaction, and who often share a feeling of social obligation towards each other (e.g. family members alone made up 46.5 per cent of seed providers in the seed flow tracer study.

Although particular types of transaction are not restricted to any one category of seed provider, it nevertheless appears that close social relations between the seed provider and receiver improve the latter's chances of preferential treatment, for example, in the type of transaction or with regards to its terms or rates.

The key role of trust in these seed transactions is directly related to the lack of transparency of seed. In addition, farmers prefer seed providers who are easy to approach and believed to be willing to grant one's request, especially if one cannot pay for the seed with money and therefore depends on negotiating another type of transaction. Finally, the trustworthiness of the seed receiver is relevant to seed providers, for instance, with regards to the types of seed transactions that involve 'payment' forms other than money, and where the seed provider depends on the seed receiver upholding his/her part of the deal.

Seed acquired from people the farmer knows and trusts is generally perceived as entailing less risk of crop failure due to inadequate seed, than seed acquired from unknown or impersonal sources, such as market vendors or commercial seed traders. In other words, the more the seed receiver knows and trusts the seed provider, the lower the perceived risk related to incomplete or incorrect information.

Finally, relations of trust are conducive to easy access to trustworthy information at low cost. Farmers may already know the characteristics of varieties used by kin or close friends, and they can easily obtain more information.

Thus, acquiring seed from social relations of trust can be seen as a way of reducing the problem of lack of transparency in seed. This, in turn, helps reduce farmers' transaction costs in relation to seed acquisition to a minimum.

Reasons for Acquiring Seed

The four main themes, motivating seed acquisition were:

(a) experimentation;

(b) to commence farming;

(c) lack of sufficient seed for planting; and

(d) initiative by other farmers.

Like farmers elsewhere, many farmers in the Central Valleys are curious and eager to learn and explore new options. While they are well aware that a maize variety that works for others may not work for them, they also recognize that other people's maize could have advantages or provide worthwhile traits. Furthermore, many farmers in the study area believe that 'foreign' seed can eventually 'acclimatize' to local conditions, if planted and selected under those conditions. These elements lead to many instances in which farmers 'try out' other materials they come across, combine them or even cross them withtheir own materials to 'see if it works'. These farmer experiments usually involve only small quantities of seed or land, thereby minimizing the risks related to experimentation. When new households start farming on their own account, they usually get seed from parents or other close relatives. Not surprisingly, therefore, this counts as an important reason for seed acquisition.

Lack of seed may be due to seed loss or to not being able or willing to save sufficient seed. Seed loss may occur because of low yield or total harvest loss, due to drought, water logging, insect attacks, weeds, hail, lodging, or poor management. Seed may be lost during storage due to insects or rodents.

A farmer may not save seed, or at least not enough, because he or she had to sell or eat everything that was harvested including the seed set aside, as a result of insufficient production, an emergency, or a crisis. Farmers who producemaize for animal feed may harvest before seed is produced. Obviously, seed loss may also occur as the result of several converging factors. People who for some reason, for instance temporary migration, decide not to plant maize for some time face a similar situation when they take up planting again, due to the relatively fast decline in maize seed germination rate and vigour.

Farmers sometimes receive seed from other farmers without having asked for it, for example, when they agree to another farmer's request for a seed-forseed exchange. Even if a farmer has not actively looked for the seed, he or she may eventually decide to plant it, although this does not always happen.

Also, farmers sometimes receive small amounts of seed as gifts. For example, one farmer's sister, who lives in another town, each year, brings small amounts of seed from her own maize field, when she comes to visit. Her brother plants this seed and explains that he regards it as a token of the affection between his sister and himself and as a way to stay 'close,' in spite of the distance that separates them. In any case, these reasons for acquiring seed are relatively infrequent.

In many cases seed loss appears to be associated with a certain social stigma, even though the cause for seed loss may be beyond the farmer's control. Informants explained that seed loss sometimes is associated with laziness, lack of knowledge, and inappropriate working practices. Meanwhile, never to have lost one's seed is a cause for pride for many farmers. Obviously, these circumstances do not motivate people to talk about the occasions on which they may have lost their seed, and it is possible that this influenced the answers to the tracer study.

Reasons for Distributing Seed

The flip side of acquiring seed is distributing it. The reasons provided by farmers for distributing seed to other farmers can be divided into two main themes:

(a) to help the recipient; and

(b) to obtain something in return, such as money or seed. where, furthermore, it was argued that access to seed in the study area may be conceptualized as part of a general social responsibility for mutual assistance.

Though most acquisitions were purchases, relatively few seed providers were motivated exclusively by obtaining money in return. This, in turn, suggests that the primary motive for farmer-to-farmer seed distribution is rarely to generate a profit. Instead, findings suggest that there is a strong cultural value in the study area associated with being helpful to others, as long as one is able to do so while covering one's own needs.

Indeed, most seed providers stated that they distributed seed to help the receiver. This fits well with the notion of 'the good farmer' and the idea that one should not refuse to help a fellow farmer asking for seed if one has sufficient seed to share. Finally, this seems to be part of a common sense of reciprocity; as one of the informants pointed out: What goes around comes around. On the other hand the frequency of purchase as transaction type and the above-mentioned broad willingness to supply seed to a buyer, also suggest that monetary gain could often be part of the motive for supplying seed.

A series of factors that influence farmers' local maize seed practices have been identified. In a number of respects, a certain similarity appears to exist across households and communities with regard to issues and frames of reference relating to maize seed practices. However, , individual households' maize seed practices are shaped by a complex mix of factors, including the interests and production conditions of each farming unit, as well as various aspects of the social, economic and physical context, and farmers' interpretations thereof. Individual households' maize seed practices should therefore be seen as the outcome of a negotiation of circumstances.

In relation to problems of seed supply, for example, householdsin the study communities negotiate solutions on an *ad hoc* basis. Similarly, although farmers in the study area have many things in common, considerable variation exists between them, even at the level of individual farmers, who on different occasions may respond differently to seemingly similar problems.

Meanwhile, at the community level, farmers' various ways of dealing with issues relating to maize seed management and supply, may, in turn, be considered to constitute a set of flexible and dynamic practices, which embrace both conservation and inncvation aspects. The terms local, informal or farmer seed system are widely understood, in the literature and among practitioners, to refer to the sets of sources of seed and related information, practices and transactional arrangements on which farmers rely to obtain seed for agricultural production.

However, the use of the term 'system' easily conveys the notion that these sets of seed sources, practices and arrangements are defined and function in a particular and tematic way. In order to avoid these somewhat deductive connotations, and to stress the flexible and dynamic characteristics of local crop genetic resource management.

The central principle of local maize seed practices in the study communities appears to be farmers' practice of selecting and saving seed from one year to another. This is the source of seed for the large majority of maize area planted in this region, and for the individual farmer this practice can help reduce perceived risk and costs. It is of further symbolic importance for some, who take pride in being self-sufficient in seed or regard the family seed as something valuable they have in trust and must pass on to subsequent generations.

In addition, the common practice of saving seed is a vital element in maintaining seed security at community level. The widespread practice of saving enough seed for the next planting, and some extra for any contingencies, provides a buffer against seed loss at the household level, but also helps ensure that, in general, seed can be obtained locally when needed.

During seed selection farmers exercise selection pressure in an attempt to enhance favoured varietal traits and lessen the influence of undesired traits. Analysis of the genetic structure of maize landraces collected in the study communities has shown a strong structure associated with farmers and communities, when phenotypic traits are analysed.

The structure of phenotypic traits indicate that varieties collected from thesame farmer or same community are more similar in their characteristics mainly ear and grain traits than those that were collected from other farmers or other villages. This indicates that human selection is playing a key role in creating and maintaining different types of maize, and hence, phenotypic diversity.

The problem of non-transparency of seed and the issue of genotype-by-environment interaction entail certain fundamental problems, which mean that acquiring maize seed is not a trivial transaction. In most cases farmers' easiest source of knowledge and trustworthy information about maize and maize seed, as well as their preferred source of seed, is people they know and trust, who in many cases also farm in the same community. Furthermore, acquiring seed from another farmer from the same community has the advantage that one knows the seed was produced in that community, and therefore is likely to be adapted to local agro-ecological conditions. Even if environmental conditions vary within the same community, in most cases, the farmer would easily be able to determine the likelihood that the seed will be adapted to the conditions of his/her own land.

Finally, using social networks to acquire seed is effective because it embeds the seed transactions in a web of obligations and, as pointed out by researchers, holds the seller's network hostage to appropriate role performance . Thus, acquiring seed via one's social network can be seen as a way of reducing the risk of planting inappropriate seed, that is, maize that does not correspond to one's production or consumption objectives, or, which is not adapted to the local environmental conditions. The notion of the 'good farmer' may also come into play in relation to maize seed transactions.

As mentioned above, it is thought appropriate 'goodfarmer- behaviour' to help other farmers in need, when possible and within reason. In as far as a farmer can spare the seed, this includes acting as seed provider on the request of other farmers who need seed. This sense of social responsibility linked to the notion of 'a good farmer' may well be triggered when a request for seed is brought forward. Meanwhile, failing to save seed is sometimes associated with a certain disgrace or loss of prestige. While this may play a role as an incentive for farmers to live up to this standard, it may also play a role in reducing the problem of free riders.

The applications and dynamics that make up the local maize seed practices in the study area appear to be grounded in a set of shared views and conditions, which in themselves are based on the agro-ecological, cultural, and social environments in which these farmers operate. Local seed supply in these communities is not based primarily on commercial motives. It is mainly part of a moral system based on trust and social responsibility.

It should be mentioned that once in a while a farmer may acquire seed at the regional market or elsewhere outside the community in order to deliberately avoid the various implications that may arise from acquiring seed from other farmers in the community; such as expectations of reciprocity and the feeling of 'indebtedness', or the 'stigma' of having lost seed. Likewise, it should be noted, that while the types of transactions not involving money payments may be attractive under some circumstances, under other circumstances a farmer may find that paying for the seed with money can provide a swift and less personal option, and thus be preferable.

When acquiring maize seed from a stranger, for instance at a regional market place, there are no means of knowing its genotype-by-environment adaptation or other characteristics apart from what the vendor claims. As several farmers exclaimed when referring to commercial traders: They just want to sell their goods! In general, acquiring seed from unknown sources is perceived by farmers as entailing a risk of acquiring inappropriate seed.

Recognizing that other maize varieties may be useful or contain desirable characteristics, farmers experiment with and 'try out' seed of other kinds of maize than their own. This allows farmers to see for themselves the traits and performance of the maize variety in question and judge whether it is appropriate for their individual needs and preferences. Meanwhile, farmers in the study communities do not associate small-scale experimentation with significant costs in terms of, for example, extra time or labour.

Theprincipal cost is the risk that the experiment will not be successful. However, this is manageable due to the small scale of most farmer experiments, which reduce the risk of major crop failure. Farmer experiments therefore serve both the purpose of information and of risk control. In addition these experiments are also used to multiply seed. If the farmer decides to incorporate the 'new' varieties into the household's maize repertoire, or alternatively mix it with seed of their own varieties in order to create new, desirable combinations, they may therefore not need to acquire seed again.

Research on the genetic structure of landraces collected in the same study communities has shown an absence of structure in these populations when neutral markers are analysed. By definition neutral markers are not under selection. They provide information on the evolutionary history of a population, including migration, bottlenecks, drift. The fact that no structure was found indicates that migration (gene flow) among these populations has been strong enough to compensate for the effects of bottlenecks and drift.

The results on genetic diversity complement the present analysis of maize seed practices in the study area. First, farmers' practice of saving and selecting seed both constitutes the basis of the phenotypic diversity observed in the study area and the foundation of local maize seed supply. One could say that each farmer is creating and maintaining his/her own unique maize varieties. Second, gene flow is important in bringing new traits and modifying varieties to fit farmers' needs as farmers do when they experiment with 'foreign'seeds, or mix them with their own.

Third, gene flow may also be important to maintain the viability of these landraces in the face of deleterious mutations, or simply to avoid inbreeding depression. In their current form, local maize seed practices allow farmers to continue this process of experimentation and incorporation of new varieties or traits into their repertoire.

Given the limited, relative frequency of seed loss in the study area, farmers' current seed supply practices appear relatively efficient in terms of maintaining local crop genetic resource diversity. While the dynamics of local seed practices depend on sufficient opportunities for obtaining seed from others when the need arises, at the moment this does not appear to be a major limitation.

From a population genetic point of view local maize seed practices appear to work well and be efficient in continuing to maintain a diversity of maize landraces and contribute to the conservation of maize genetic diversity.

Farmers' demand for seed of other types of maize is relatively infrequent, and mostly involves relatively small amounts of seed. Under these circumstances supplying seed may not be a profitable enterprise.

Interventions such as those practised in the CIMMYT/INIFAP research project demonstrated farmers' interest in acquiring seed of other maize varieties. However, the average quantity of seed per acquisition was just 4.3 kg, which may not be a problem if the demand is only for one or two varieties. However, if the demand is for many different types of maize, the costs of producing, managing and selling seed may be too high for a commercial provider, since commercial seed enterprises most likely have to supply larger quantities of fewer varieties to be financially viable. This is an issue which merits further investigation.

Maize continues to play an important role in the study area in terms of food security. While farmers in these communities are often curious and interested in trying out new things, in many cases, they are also concerned about risks in relation to their maize production.

Unstable seed supply, timeliness of seed supply, higher costs of improved seed - in the study area approximately 5-7 times the cost of farmer saved seed - all add to the more generic problem of non-transparency of seed, and could influence and hamper the adoption process. Under such circumstances one would expect farmers first to experiment for some time with small quantities of seed, before deciding whether or not to adopt.

To a large extent many of these challenges lead back to the fundamental problem of non-transparency of seed, and to the importance of trustworthy information about maize seed of different varieties. Identifying ways of conveying the relevant information to the users of the seed in a straightforward and trustworthy way would seem a useful contribution in this regard. Further research is needed on how to achieve this.

Despite a strong concern for risk avoidance, farmer interest in and willingness to experiment and learn about new and different maize types, presents an opportunity for the introduction of improved germplasm. Though this experimentation mostly involves small quantities of seed, it nevertheless presents a window of opportunity for the introduction of alternative maize germplasm. Many farmers in the study communities express an attitude of generalized trust in other farmers and farmer-to-farmer information flows can play an important role in relation to the spread of information regarding innovations and new technologies.

One opportunity could be to explore how this could be used actively in relation to seed and information about seed and other technologies. The concept of 'farmer-dealers' was for example an important element in the spread of hybrid maize in the US. By using local farmers as their agents, seed companies andgovernment extension agencies promoted their products through local channels that farmers felt comfortable with and could easily relate to.

In the study reported on here, no specialized seed-focused institutions of collective action were identified. Interventions based on collective action to support farmers' efforts to maintain maize diversity in this region, such as establishing community seed banks, may therefore not be successful. Initiatives directed more towards individual farmers, such as the CIMMYT/INIFAP research project, or which build on local institutions that serve other purposes, may be more effective.

Rather than maintaining specialized networks for seed needs, which occur relatively infrequent, farmers tend to 'piggy-back' seed needs on other networks of social relations on an *ad hoc* basis. The problem of non-transparency of seed is one of the factors, which may influence the decision to transact with a friend or a relative, as a response to the perceived risk or uncertainty this fosters. Under these circumstances, development interventions at the community level, whether directed towards conservation or introduction of improved seed, should focus on existing social organisations rather than trying to create new organisations dedicated to seed supply.

Bibliography

Pressoir, G. and Berthaud, J. (2004). Population Structure and Strong Divergent Selection Shape Phenotypic Diversification in Maize Landraces. *Heredity,* 92(2): 95-101.

Pretty, J. and Smith, D. (2004). Social Capital in Biodiversity Conservation and Management. *Conservation Biology*, 18 (3): 631-63.

Putnam, R.D. (1993). The Prosperous Community. Social Capital and Public Life. *The American Prospect*, 4 (13).

Putnam, R.D. (1995). Bowling Alone: America's Declining Social Capital. *Journal of Democracy,* 6 (1): 65-78.

Putnam, R.D. (1996). The Strange Disappearance of Civic America. *The American Prospect*, 7 (24).

Quiroz, C. (1996). Local Knowledge Systems Contribute to Sustainable Development. *Indigenous Knowledge Monitor* 4 (1).

Rack, M. (2003). Interfaces of Knowledge: The Revival of Temples in West Hunan, China. In: Pottier, J.; Bicker, A.; Sillitoe, P. (Eds.), *Negotiating Local Knowledge. Power and Identity in Development.* Pluto Press. London. Sterling,Virginia.

Ravnborg, H. Munk (1993). Targeting International Agricultural Research Towards the Rural Poor. *CDR Working Paper, 93.4.* Centre for Development Research, Copenhagen.

Ravnborg, H. Munk (1996). *Agricultural Research and the Peasants. The Tanzanian Agricultural Knowledge and Information System.* Centre forDevelopment Research, Copenhagen.

Ravnborg, H.M.; Cruz, A.M. de la; Guerrero, M.P.; Westermann, O. (2002).Collective Action in Ant Control. In: Meinzen-Dick, R.; Knox, A.; Place, F.;Swallow, B. (Eds.), *Innovation in Natural Resource Management. The Role of Property Rights and Collective Action in Developing Countries.* Johns Hopkins University Press. pp. 257-271.

Remington, T.; Walsh, S.; Charles, E.; Maroko, J.; Omanga, P. (2002). Getting Off the Seeds-and-Tools Treadmill with CRS Seed Vouchers and Fairs.*Disasters,* 26 (4): 316-328.

Rice, E.; Smale, M.; Blanco, J. L. (1998). Farmers' Use of Improved Seed Selection Practices in Mexican Maize: Evidence and Issues from the Sierra deSanta Marta. *World Development,* 26 (9): 1625-1640.

Richards, P. (1985). *Indigenous Agricultural Revolution: Ecology and Food Productionin West Africa.* Hutchinson, London and Westview Press, Boulder.

Richards, P. (1989). Agriculture as a Performance. In: Chambers, R.; Pacey, A.; Thrupp, L.A. (Eds.) *Farmer First: Farmer Innovation and Agricultural Research.* Intermediate Technology Publications Ltd., London, UK.

Ritchie, S.W. and Hanway, J. J. (1982). *How a Corn Plant Develops.* Special Report No. 48. Iowa State University of Science and Technology. Cooperative Extension Service, Ames, Iowa.

Ritzer, G. and Goodman, D.J. (2003). *Sociological Theory.* 6th Edition. McGraw-Hill, New York.

Roberts, B.R. (2001). The New Social Policies in Latin America and the Development of Citizenship: An Interface Perspective. Paper for Workshopon Agency, Knowledge and Power: New Directions. Wageningen 14th-15th December.

Rohrbach, D.D. (1997). Farmer-to-farmer Seed Movements in Zimbabwe: Issues Arising. In: Rohrbach, D.D.; Bishaw, Z.; Gastel, A.J.G. van (Eds.), *Alternative Strategies for Smallholder Seed Supply*. Proceedings of an International Conference on Options for Strengthening National and Regional Seed Systems in Africa and West Asia. March 1997, Harare, Zimbabwe. ICRISAT, India.

Rosaldo, M.Z. (1974). Woman, Culture and Society: A Theoretical Overview. In: Rosaldo, M. and Lamphere, L. (Eds.), *Woman, Culture and Society*. Standford University Press, California.

Rose-Ackerman, S. (2001). Trust, Honesty and Corruption: Reflections on the State-building Process. *Arch. Europ. Sociol.*, XLII (3): 526-570.

Rothstein, B. (2000). Trust, Social Dilemmas and Collective Memories. *Journal of Theoretical Politics*, 12 (4): 477-501.

Rucht, D. (2002). Summary of the Main Results and Identification of Research Questions. Discussant's Comments. Cultural Diversity, Collective Identity and Collective Action - Consequences of the Opening up of National Borders, ESF Forward Look Workshop, April 2002, Italy.

Ruiz Garcia, Aida (2002). *Migración Oaxaquena. Una aproximación a la realidad.* Coordinación Estatal de Atención al Migrante Oaxaqueno. Oaxaca, Mexico.

Sahlins, M.D. (1968). Tribal Economics. In Sahlins, M.D.: *Tribesmen.* Englewood Cliffs, New Jersey.

Sahlins, M.D. (1972). *Stone Age Economics.* Aldine Publ. Co., New York, USA. Salvador, R.J. (undated). Maize. Adaptation of an Article Originally Published in *The Encyclopedia of Mexico: History, Culture and Society*, 1997, Fitzroy Dearborn Publishers.

Sánchez, J.J.G.; Goodman, M.M.; Stuber, C.W. (2000b). Isoenzymatic and Morphological Diversity in the Races of Maize in Mexico. *Economic Botany* 54: 43-59.

Index